THE NEK

GW00778696

ANZAC BATTLES SERIES

Series Editor: Glyn Harper

The Anzac Battles Series is a collection of books describing the great military battles fought by Australian and New Zealand soldiers during the wars of the twentieth century. Each title in the series focuses on one battle, describing the background to the action, the combat itself, the strategy employed and the outcome. The story is told through the actions of the main protagonists and the individuals who distinguished themselves in the battle. The authors are all respected military historians with specialist knowledge of the battles described.

ANZAC BATTLES SERIES

Series Editor: Glyn Harper

THE NEK
A GALLIPOLI TRAGEDY

PETER BURNESS

Pen & Sword
MILITARY

First published in New Zealand in 1996
by Exisle Publishing Limited

First published in Great Britain in 2013 by
PEN & SWORD MILITARY
An imprint of
Pen & Sword Books Ltd
47 Church Street
Barnsley
South Yorkshire
S70 2AS

ISBN 978 1 78159 307 3

Printed and bound in England
By CPI Group (UK) Ltd, Croydon, CR0 4YY

Pen & Sword Books Ltd incorporates the Imprints of Pen & Sword Aviation,
Pen & Sword Family History, Pen & Sword Maritime, Pen & Sword Military,
Pen & Sword Discovery, Pen & Sword Politics, Pen & Sword Archaeology,
Pen & Sword Atlas, Wharncliffe Local History, Wharncliffe True Crime,
Wharncliffe Transport, Pen & Sword Select, Pen & Sword Military Classics,
Leo Cooper, The Praetorian Press, Claymore Press, Remember When,
Seaforth Publishing and Frontline Publishing

For a complete list of Pen & Sword titles please contact
PEN & SWORD BOOKS LIMITED
47 Church Street, Barnsley, South Yorkshire, S70 2AS, England
E-mail: enquiries@pen-and-sword.co.uk
Website: www.pen-and-sword.co.uk

CONTENTS

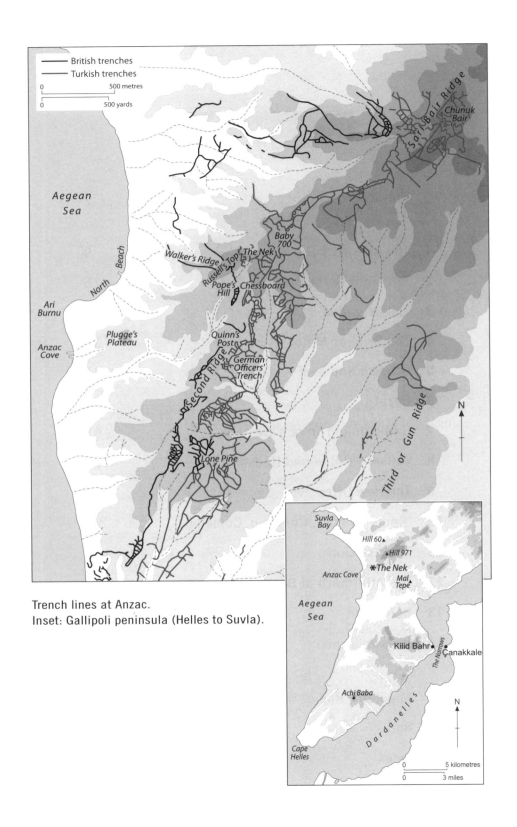

- British trenches
- Turkish trenches

0 ——— 500 metres
0 ——— 500 yards

Aegean Sea

Sari Bair Ridge

Chunuk Bair

North Beach

Walker's Ridge

Russell's Top

The Nek

Baby 700

Pope's Hill

Chessboard

Ari Burnu

Plugge's Plateau

Anzac Cove

Quinn's Post

Second Ridge

German Officers' Trench

Lone Pine

Third or Gun Ridge

N

Trench lines at Anzac.
Inset: Gallipoli peninsula (Helles to Suvla).

Suvla Bay

Hill 60

Hill 971

Anzac Cove

*The Nek

Mal Tepe

Aegean Sea

Kilid Bahr

The Narrows

Çanakkale

Achi Baba

Dardanelles

Cape Helles

0 ——— 5 kilometres
0 ——— 3 miles

N

My long-held interest in the events described in this book probably developed from a familiarity with George Lambert's famous painting, *The Charge of the 3rd Light Horse Brigade at The Nek*, and the sad relics of the battle displayed in the Australian War Memorial. Having, over the years, collected information from major and obscure sources, often only brief references, I eventually decided that there was sufficient material for a book.

The first edition of *The Nek* appeared in 1996 and at that time I expressed my sympathy for all those men, of all ranks, who found themselves on, or near, that terrible battlefield on 7 August 1915. By publishing an account of the battle, I felt that I had joined the storytellers who, over the years, had kept alive the memory of the tragedy. Since then others have written on the topic. All of this has helped ensure that these men's stories are not forgotten.

I was fortunate in 1984 to have had the opportunity to interview a handful of old soldiers who had been at The Nek on that tragic day. Their accounts provided a unique dimension to my study. As the decades passed, that generation of men departed. None are now left, and I realise more than ever what a remarkable privilege it was to hear their accounts. Those veteran Anzacs included the late Lionel Simpson DCM, who was the last survivor of the charge.

From the beginning, and extending to the present time, I have been helped and encouraged by many people, some of whom are mentioned in the notes. I have not attempted to mention all those who have helped for fear of missing out many. Management, colleagues and staff at the Memorial have made my work possible, and those individuals and families who gave me access to family papers and other information deserve my special thanks. It was particularly important for me to discover the private papers of Lieutenant Colonel Alexander White, the officer who died leading the charge, and to be given permission to use them. I have also enjoyed the exchange of details with other historians and writers who have tackled this subject. The De Lambert Largesse Foundation generously provided the resources for me to extend my study in this and other topics.

Anyone researching Australian participation in the First World War owes a great debt to Charles Bean, and I am no exception. I drew inspiration and knowledge from his published volumes, and from his diaries and correspondence preserved at the Australian War Memorial. My account of the battle may add detail and background, but it does nothing to undermine the authority of the description he presented in his second volume of the Official History of Australia in the War of 1914–18. Among modern scholars of the battle, Jeff Pickerd offered useful comments.

This edition of the book contains some additions and amendments. Although I have gathered some more descriptions of the battle, I have been circumspect in incorporating these into the text, preferring mostly to retain the existing construction of the original book. I truly hope that I have represented everyone fairly and honestly.

The battle for The Nek has become an important part of the story of Australia at war. Its place within the Anzac legend was reinforced by the film *Gallipoli*, which still retains a wide popularity after all these years, and by the retelling of the battle in more recent publications. But it is too easy to forget that many lives were lost, men were maimed and reputations suffered. This is a story that deserves to be remembered.

Peter Burness
Australian War Memorial, Canberra
May 2012

CHAPTER 1

The Attack at The Nek

Battles often begin in the dimness before dawn, or in the evening around sunset. First light on 7 August 1915 was to be the test for the Australians in the 3rd Light Horse Brigade on Gallipoli. On that morning they were to make a dismounted charge across the narrow no-man's-land which had separated them and the Turks for the past 12 weeks. Most of the light horsemen did not show alarm at the task they had been set. Among many there was nervous anticipation, for this was to be their first real taste of pitched battle, and it would be a demonstration of their worth. They were aware that the infantrymen, who had got a tenuous grip on the peninsula when they made their amphibious landing in April, were watching to see how well these more recently arrived troops, supposedly Australia's elite, would acquit themselves.

There was a strong belief that this was to be the brigade's climactic battle, from which victory would come. In the network of trenches, and in the saps which had been driven beyond the ragged front line, men waited for the order to charge. Most had been sitting quietly through the previous day and night, sometimes managing to snatch a few moments of uneasy sleep. The collective air of excitement concealed the natural fear and concern of individuals. All their training, travel and hardships had brought them to this moment. They were willing and confident, and by now the opportunity to participate in a great battle seemed a part of the natural course of their lives.

The sounds of war were all around them. This was part of a large-scale general movement. Actions had commenced on the previous evening, and all night the noise of fighting drifted across from the flanks. After some hours the tap, tap, tap of machine-guns, and the pop of rifle-fire, softened by the distance, began to die away, only to return as fighting ebbed and flowed. Later came the sharp swish overhead, followed by the nearby crash of a shell-burst on the enemy trenches opposite as the artillery began its preparation for the dawn attack.

The darkness had brought relief from the heat of the day, but the night was cold. The men were only thinly dressed, so some went down to the communications trenches to help themselves to the greatcoats which had been piled with others' belongings. They reckoned that things could be sorted out again later. About 3 am a staff sergeant, with a small party carrying stone jars, began to move about distributing a double issue of rum.

Each man knew that shortly he would confront the enemy, armed with only the bayonet on his rifle, while a few carried hand bombs. Ammunition hung heavily in pouches worn above the waist, but all rifles were unloaded, for this was to be a bayonet assault. Hopefully the Turks would not stand and fight. If they did it was going to be a vicious and bloody melee. It was not a thought to dwell on; most men were silently concerned only that their courage would not be seen to fail.

The Turks' earthworks looked formidable. The Australians were on a feature called Russell's Top, facing the Sari Bair Range, which was held by the enemy. Joining these was a bridge of land called The Nek. Here the Turks had their trenches, extending back in rows up the hill behind, called Baby 700.

At 4 am the allied artillery began to concentrate on the forward slopes of Baby 700. Fire from the Royal Navy standing off-shore joined in. It was the heaviest bombardment the light horsemen had seen, and they were reassured to see shells bursting on the enemy, throwing up dirt, dust and smoke, which drifted heavily across into their own lines. In the soft light a veil of yellow smoke gathered over the Turks, leaving only their foremost trenches visible. For half an hour the shell-fire grew in intensity. Then it stopped.

The moment for the attack had arrived. In the front line, formed of deep trenches and shallow saps, the first wave of attacking troops waited for an agonising seven minutes for the order, which was to come from the commanding officer of the 8th Light Horse. Lieutenant Colonel Alexander White had been keen and fresh-faced when he arrived on Gallipoli. He was now anxious and tired, and his sun helmet concealed the nasty shrapnel wound, which had put him in hospital just a few weeks earlier. Finally, he yelled 'Go!' The order was passed along the line and 150 men, with White at their front, clambered up, with their bayonets fixed, to face the enemy.

The Australians rushed forward across the rough ground to be met by a gale of flying metal. Quickly, hundreds of rifles from directly opposite were joined by machine-guns higher up the slopes, snapping out fire. In the dimness the flames from the rifle barrels seemed to spit halfway across no-man's-land. The sound of the shooting engulfed the battlefield, smothering the ferocious yells of the attackers and the screams and moans of those hit. The Turkish riflemen fired furiously. Their shots tore and smashed through bone and flesh. They saw the Australians dropping, not singly, but in dozens. Within a couple of minutes there was only a scattered handful left.

Then, against the backdrop of a dark sea, another line of attackers rose. A row of widely-spaced leaders first appeared, closely followed by their troops. Again more than 150 men scrambled forward yelling, with their bayonets thrust before them. In a moment they too were falling. The volume of rifle and machine-gun fire was enormous. Against this, men had no chance. Almost everyone was hit, many even before they had found their footing after clambering from the trench.

The dead and wounded soon littered the battlefield. The brigade had lost one of its regiments in just five minutes. The men of the second line had not even got as far as the first. In some places a few of the wounded scrambled for better cover, while several of the immobile were helped by mates. Sergeant Henry Nugent of the 8th Regiment, a survivor who had sought some protection after being shot through the hand, later described the charge in a letter to his mother:

> It was grand to see the spirit in which the boys went over the top of that trench at the word of command. Every man knew that he was going to almost certain death, but not one hesitated. We had only 40 yards to go to the Turkish trenches, but not one man reached them. Our men fell dead and wounded 10 yards from the goal. It was just hell, and no man could penetrate and live.[1]

Movement had almost ceased 15 minutes after the assault began, and the firing was beginning to die down. Already it was becoming light. It was apparent that the attack had been decisively defeated. Certainly, nobody expected that the Australians would maintain their action. However, at 4.45 am a third line of light horsemen sprang forth. These were the Western

Australians of the 10th Light Horse Regiment. They had filed into the front trenches after the previous two waves left. Dead and wounded were already choking the trenches and, although they had not been able to look over the parapet, the Western Australians could hear the devastating firepower they were to face. But the order was given, and they obeyed.

The Western Australians' efforts were doomed. Even if they could reach the enemy's trenches, the loss of the previous two lines meant that they would not have the strength to take and hold any of them. The Turks were now fully alert and again met the assault with withering fire, which had been joined by artillery bursting its shrapnel over no-man's-land. The third line was simply swept away.

The battle could have ended there. However, further tragedy was heaped upon folly. At 5.15 am a fourth line, this time smaller than the others, made a final charge. This futile assault, which could not hope to achieve anything, was almost destroyed on its own parapet. It took only a few minutes for the fighting to be over. The Australians' hopes had been extinguished.

Two hundred and forty men were killed, and about 140 wounded, in this short, sharp action. In the trenches, from which they had begun only minutes earlier, there was shock and chaos. Some officers and a few men peered out over the battlefield, using periscopes, looking in disbelief at the fate of their two fine regiments. Around them the dead lay on the dirt floor. Several already had coats thrown over their faces to hide the horror they presented. A few of the mortally injured were passing their final moments in agony. The other wounded were beginning to receive some treatment, and stretcher-bearers had started moving them away. The evacuation system was soon overwhelmed. Unless they were strong enough to pass the rest of the day unattended, they had little chance of survival.

Dead and wounded lay thick in no-man's-land. For many, death had been instantaneous. Others were wounded and isolated, with neither the strength nor the opportunity to get back. Among the suffering, some prayed – weeks later a body was recovered still grasping a prayer book – while others called in vain for help. Those who could crawled in carefully, and for at least an hour there was a slow stream of men slipping over the parapet. Several who had found some cover were pinned down. They waited through the day until darkness before making their dash for safety.

The battle for The Nek had ended. In the front trenches things were in a shambles, and the battlefield appeared crowded with the dead and dying. Charles Bean wrote that, 'as the sun of that burning day climbed higher … movement ceased. Over the whole summit the figures lay still in the quivering heat.'[2] In the next few days attention would be drawn to the fighting elsewhere, although not far away. But no major gains could be made there either.

The Australians never did take The Nek. The failure of the attacks launched here, and elsewhere, in August was an indicator that nothing more was possible at Anzac. Finally, in December, the allies withdrew, slipping away quietly before the Turks realised they had gone. As the Australians left, perhaps in spite as much as in defiance, they detonated a huge mine under the enemy's front trench at The Nek. The explosion was a signal that the campaign here was over.

The story of the charge at The Nek became part of the history of Australia's experience at war, both as fact and as mythology. Early accounts tended to focus on the heroic efforts of those who had lost their lives, and on the courage that they had displayed in going willingly to their deaths for the greater cause.

Charles Bean published his final volume of the Official History of Australia in the War of 1914–18 in 1942, ending, at least in one sense, a task he had commenced 28 years earlier. When he came to his last chapter, he was compelled to say something about the discipline of the Australian Imperial Force. He wrote:

> In the history of war there is no more signal example of reckless obedience than that given by the dismounted light horsemen at The Nek when, after seeing the whole of the first attacking line mown down within a few yards by a whirlwind of rifle and machine-gun fire, the second, third, and fourth lines each charged after its interval of time, at the signal of its leaders, to certain destruction.[3]

Comparisons with the charge of the Light Brigade, a famous cavalry action during the Crimean War, and an inspiring story of Victorian valour known to all of the First World War generation since childhood, were inevitable. Even participants and the historian Charles Bean could not avoid the analogy. The connection remained strong and, in the 1930s, a prestigious Australian War Memorial publication said that 'the charge of the six hundred British cavalry against the Russian guns at Balaclava immortalised in Alfred

Lord Tennyson's stirring poem "The Charge of the Light Brigade", had its counterpart at the Anzac "Nek".[4] Indeed, Tennyson's words do seem most apt:

> They that had fought so well
> Came through the jaws of Death,
> Back from the mouth of Hell,
> All that was left of them,
> Left of six hundred.

Yet behind the glorious charge of the Light Brigade there is a story of inadequacies, incompetence and bitter personal rivalries. The action at The Nek was no different. The attack had been a disaster. Hundreds of lives had been lost needlessly, and for no gain. The Australians had been set a task that was unachievable and, even when this was apparent following the destruction of the first line, three more waves were sent to the same fate.

Something had gone very seriously wrong at The Nek. The courage of the officers and men who made the charge cannot be denied. We can only join Bean in admiring their remarkable discipline. But battles cannot be fought solely on the basis of discipline and courage. It was in the other skills and qualities – most particularly those sought in certain leaders – that the conduct of this battle was deficient. The terrible waste of human life was a consequence of these failures.

CHAPTER 2

3rd Light Horse Brigade

The 3rd Australian Light Horse Brigade was not yet a year old when it faced its trial on Gallipoli. It had been formed in 1914, several weeks after the outbreak of war. On 4 August Great Britain had declared herself, and consequently the forces of her Empire, to be at war with Germany. In anticipation of this, Australia had been quick to offer her small navy and a volunteer army to assist, and on 6 August, this offer was accepted with a request that the force be prepared quickly. No one could then foresee how long and devastating this war would be, so initially a single division of infantry and one brigade of light horse, to be named the Australian Imperial Force – soon to be known simply by the initials 'AIF' – was prepared.

Although it drew on the former peacetime army for its first batch of officers and non-commissioned officers (NCOs), the AIF had to be a new, distinct and entirely volunteer force. The existing home army was based on compulsory part-time service for all young men. However, this militia was intended only to fight in the nation's defence and, in any case, the scheme was still in its infancy. Any hope that currently serving regiments would be accepted intact had to be dismissed. Barracks and drill halls opened to take the names of those now willing to enlist in the new national expeditionary force.

Men joining the AIF who could ride had a natural preference for the light horse over the infantry. The light horse was more selective and it had associations with military dash, together with the perceived characteristics of ruggedness and individuality, and the rural virtues of resource and mateship. Also, following the South African War, in which most of the Australians had served on horseback, the mounted regiments had a tradition and a good record in battle. As a consequence, more men sought to join the light horse than could at first be accepted.

The first division was quickly formed. The accompanying light horse brigade was made up of a regiment from New South Wales, one from Queensland, and another drawn jointly from South Australia and Queensland. A fourth regiment was raised in Victoria as divisional cavalry. On 3 September it was announced that Australia's contribution would be expanded and arrangements were made to provide a second contingent. As a result, another light horse brigade was quickly raised and, as the expansion continued, a third brigade followed in October. Australia's contribution would continue to grow, calling on more and more men to join up.

Victoria, South Australia and Western Australia supplied the men for the 3rd Light Horse Brigade. When the second brigade was being brought together, it was thought that Queensland and Victoria would each provide a second regiment and that the remaining one would be a joint contribution from South Australia and Western Australia. But once it was evident that there were sufficient willing men to have New South Wales provide two more whole regiments and another from Western Australia, it was decided to use the Western Australians, South Australians and the men still available in Victoria to form the third brigade under the command of Colonel Frederic Hughes, a Victorian, on the following basis:

8th Light Horse Regiment   – Victoria
9th Light Horse Regiment   – South Australia
                             (with one squadron from Victoria)
10th Light Horse Regiment – Western Australia

The light horse was not a cavalry force, nor was it, as sometimes described, made up of infantrymen on horseback. It was a force of trained and skilled horsemen who could fight dismounted. The light horseman's mount gave him mobility, but in action he would dismount to fight on foot; in battle, one man in four was usually required to be a horse-holder. A light horse regiment was not nearly as strong as a battalion of infantry, and a troop had nothing like the firepower of a platoon. On the other hand, it was a highly mobile and flexible body, could travel distances, and also do some of the work traditionally given to cavalry, such as patrolling, reconnaissance and screening the main force.

Each brigade of three regiments included its own signal troop, field ambulance, machine-guns and transport. The basic unit was the troop (itself composed of small sections) consisting usually of one officer and 35 other ranks. Four troops made up a squadron, and three squadrons, plus a machine-gun section and headquarters, made up a regiment.

The early volunteers in Victoria were sent to a camp established in open paddocks at Broadmeadows outside Melbourne. The site was about two and a half kilometres from the railway station and lacked even a water supply until army engineers were able to extend a pipeline. Eventually tens of thousands of troops would pass through this camp. The first mounted men to go there were destined for the 4th Light Horse Regiment. The overflow volunteers for the 4th were drafted into an area at the eastern end of the camp and divided into training squadrons, each of about 150 men. Here they were put through their preliminary training and dismounted drill. In October they were formed into a second Victorian regiment, under the command of Lieutenant Colonel Alexander White. The regiment, the 8th Light Horse, moved its camp over beside that of the 4th, whose grounds it took over when that regiment departed.

The scene at Broadmeadows was repeated at camps of the 9th and 10th Regiments outside Adelaide and Perth. Together, South Australia and Tasmania had provided men for the 3rd Regiment and there had been two senior Adelaide officers, both with service in the South African War and currently with militia regiments, available for that command. The appointment was given to Lieutenant Colonel Frank Rowell, while the other officer, Albert Miell, was to be his second-in-command. When it was decided that further light horse regiments were to be formed, Miell was retained to command one. He was a natural choice when the new South Australian regiment (the 9th Light Horse) became available.

At first it was thought that Western Australia could provide just a squadron, and many disappointed horsemen there were directed to the infantry. Lieutenant Colonel Noel Brazier, who commanded the state's only militia light horse regiment, had enough of his own officers and men wanting to transfer to the AIF that he had no trouble achieving the required numbers for the squadron. He was prepared to drop his rank if necessary to lead it. With the decision made that the contribution would be expanded and a complete regiment would be supplied, Brazier undertook to raise and command it. The original squadron had already gone into camp at Guildford outside Perth, where it was joined by the new ones after they finished their initial training.

Western Australians had already played a useful role in the South African War. The state boasted sending a higher number of mounted men, proportionate to its population, to that war than any other. Its citizen force light horse regiment was descended from the former Western Australian Mounted Infantry, and in 1912 it was named the 25th Light Horse. When the war started, almost half of the serving officers sought to join the AIF, and several of them were accepted into the 10th Light Horse.

The volunteers from South Australia were medically examined and went into camp at Morphettville, where they were put through their riding tests. After some training they paraded through Adelaide before moving by train to Melbourne, where they were joined by the local squadron in camp at Broadmeadows.

In the early months of the war there was no shortage of willing recruits. Australian-born and immigrants, bushmen and city clerks, professional men and street larrikins all found their way into the AIF, attracted by the prospect of adventure, comradeship, overseas travel and adult pay, and by the reassurance that their countrymen had declared this war to be a noble and just cause.

Some men were remarkable for their efforts to get into the AIF. In the west one young man rode over 500 kilometres to Wyndham to catch a boat for Fremantle to find a recruiting office. He was taken into the 10th Light Horse. Walter McConnan, a 28-year-old Australian, was touring Britain when the war broke out. He was well-educated and considered seeking a commission in a British regiment, but decided to come home. He joined the 8th Light Horse in camp. Before returning he had written to his father:

> I was nearly into the army for the term of the war last week. I cabled Melbourne for permission and got it but on further consideration thought it wiser to return next week and if it is necessary go with the Australian forces with your approval. I have no desire for the life but what can one do in the face of the 'call to arms'. It seems that the only thing which will bring the war to a speedy end is the landing on the Continent of a huge trained force. It is quite a usual thing for fellows like myself to go off to some or other regiment as privates.[1]

Soldiering had greater appeal to Douglas Bethune, a Boer War veteran, already over 30, who was one of two brothers also accepted into the 8th Regiment. He explained his reasons for joining up: 'I am not overcome with patriotic fervour and the desire is purely selfish. I'd give anything for the excitement of it all again.'² With his experience he did not expect any problem in getting promotion.

Early training at Broadmeadows was limited to rifle drill, bayonet practice, physical exercises, lectures, guards, piquets, and excursions to the Williamstown rifle range for shooting. Men slept on straw-filled palliasses and in their free time mixed at the newly opened garrison institute, visited friends in neighbouring units, or perhaps went to the camp photographer's tented studio to have a final portrait taken. Visitors were often allowed into the camp. In the second week of November the horses arrived, and the men felt that at last they were truly mounted soldiers.

Quickly the men were transformed from civilians. The first uniforms issued were shapeless blue cotton-drill jackets and trousers and floppy white hats for work around the camp. Civilian clothes were sent home or handed in to the Salvation Army. Eventually proper service dress was received. The uniform for the light horse was workmanlike and not very different from that worn by the infantry. Both had the loose comfortably fitting woollen jacket with breeches, with slight variations in the latter. What did make the horsemen distinctive were their spurs and polished leather leggings, belts, pouches and bandoliers. The 3rd Light Horse Brigade also wore the slouch hat, topped with plumes of emu feathers. The plumes mostly appeared on parades and had previously been associated with the Queenslanders. In the following years most other light horse regiments followed the brigade's example, and the plume became an admired symbol of the light horse.

The light horseman was expected to fight on foot, and so his main weapon was the rifle rather than the sword, lance or carbine of the cavalry. Although they served on Gallipoli without their horses, it was not a role they liked. One of the brigade's officers was to express his concern at the change: 'In doing this we are giving everything. For [us] to go as infantry is a great sacrifice.'³ Above all else, they still prided themselves on being horsemen.

The light horseman's service rifle was modern and accurate. Following the war in South Africa, the British army decided that one firearm was needed for both the infantry and mounted troops, removing the distinction between rifle and carbine and providing a weapon which was shorter, lighter and faster to load than the Lee-Enfields then in use. The Short Magazine Lee-Enfield (SMLE) was the result, and this sturdy bolt-action rifle was eventually to serve the Australian soldier in two world wars and Korea. It fired .303-inch rounds, which were loaded into a magazine using clips, or charges, of five rounds each. These were carried in bandoliers slung across the shoulders and in leather pouches on belts. The shorter length SMLE was compensated for by its having a bayonet with a 43-centimetre blade.

Training and camp routine became more strenuous in the last several weeks leading up to Christmas. Mounted cross-country work provided an opportunity for men and horses to become familiar with military commands and movements. Officers and NCOs attended special courses and sat examinations. Groups now began to move as troops, to act as part of a squadron and to understand their place within the regiment, while most of the misfits had already been discharged or had deserted.

Trooper McConnan provided some insight into camp life in a letter home:

Every evening finds me tired and every meal time I am hungry. Most of last week was spent at Williamstown for shooting. We left here at 6 am and got back at 6 pm. Long days! We had the usual tedious church parade ... it is a good sight to see the various regiments march up with bands playing. Our daily programme will be quite different now the horses are here. There is more work but now we feel more like a mounted regiment. The food is not at all bad. We get roasts occasionally – Bread and jam with tea is the usual 5.30 bill of fare; last night they gave cheese instead of jam [and] one can buy butter and milk.[4]

More efforts seem to have been made within the 3rd Light Horse Brigade than in most others to develop a pride and an identity; the plumed slouch hat was just one demonstration of this. Both the 9th and 10th Regiments held public parades at which handsome embroidered unit flags or unofficial 'colours' were accepted from the local citizens. The 8th Regiment sought a distinctive appearance with its horses: the chestnuts went to A Squadron, the bays and light browns to B, and the dark browns and blacks to C. The regiment also formed a mounted band; something rarely seen in Australia. The officers went further, having tailored uniforms made and unofficial enamelled badges struck.

It was unfortunate that the 8th Light Horse, which started with such high hopes, should end the war with a reputation as an unlucky regiment. Jack Dean, who joined upon its formation as an 18-year-old, was interviewed

70 years later. He still recalled his old regiment with affection: 'It was a particularly good one, well formed with good officers. A very good lot. But they had more than their fair share of disasters.'[5] He was right. The 8th suffered the most severely at The Nek, and fared little better in the later campaigns in the Middle East. It had more casualties in the course of the war than any other light horse unit; the losses included its three commanding officers.

By the end of 1914 the brigade, minus the 10th Regiment, was concentrated at Broadmeadows, ready to be sent overseas. The 9th Light Horse had arrived from South Australia in pouring rain, and the wet weather continued through December, frustrating the training, making living in tents uncomfortable, and turning the lines into avenues of mud. Major Carew Reynell of the 9th Regiment, recently arrived from an officers' course, reported the appearance of a general 'fedupness' and complained that it was 'impossible to preserve any proper standard of personal cleanliness or smartness of turnout'.[6] This mood quickly passed as Christmas approached and most of the men were given leave to spend some time with family and friends.

In Western Australia the 10th Light Horse marched mounted and fully equipped through Perth to a camp at the Agricultural Society's showground at Claremont, where a public review and sports day was held. The citizens turned out to see their state's only AIF light horse regiment. When the men returned from the Christmas–New Year leave they were sent to a new camp at Rockingham, south of Perth. A month later the regiment made its last move, back to the dusty camp at Claremont.

The brigade was now fully formed, had undergone its basic training, and was anxiously waiting to be sent overseas to the front. The early volunteers for the AIF had imagined that they would soon be fighting the Germans in France, but events took a different twist. While the first contingent was at sea, news was received that it would not go to Britain but instead land and stay in Egypt, where the Australians and New Zealanders would be formed into a corps and placed under the command of Lieutenant General Sir William Birdwood.

An Indian-born Englishman, Birdwood had attended the Royal Military College, Sandhurst, and been first commissioned in 1885. He served as a staff officer in numerous Indian frontier campaigns and the South African War, where he became a favourite of Lord Kitchener, Britain's imperial hero and now Secretary of State for War. His appointment to command the

AIF was fortunate both for his career and for the Australians, with whom he developed a unique and enduring relationship. After the war he returned to the Indian army and ultimately, in 1925, attained the rank of field marshal.

The change of destination for the Australians had been caused by a delay in constructing suitable camp accommodation in Britain, and by the entry of Turkey into the war and the consequent threat to Egypt. By mid-December the last units of the first contingent had landed and gone into Mena Camp, outside Cairo. The men of the second contingent could now expect that they too would be sent to Egypt. The destiny of the 3rd Light Horse Brigade was set.

CHAPTER 3

The Brigadier

The light horse brigade's operations at The Nek had been under the direct command of Colonel Frederic Hughes. It was perhaps inevitable that he would later bear much of the blame for the failure of the attack and the consequent heavy casualties. Several weeks after the battle, he became ill and was evacuated from the peninsula. He was not allowed to return to the front, and instead was sent back to Australia. He protested, but it was no good; he was never again given a fighting command.

Hughes was not a regular officer but a citizen-soldier who had given a large part of his spare time over many years to military training. A colonel commanding a militia light horse brigade in Victoria when the war started, he was already known to several of the officers in the 8th Light Horse who had served under him, or through their city or club connections. He had not commanded men in action until he arrived on Gallipoli.

Hughes had been accepted for the AIF despite his age. He was approaching 57 when appointed to raise and command the 3rd Light Horse Brigade. With almost 40 years of service as an artilleryman, light horseman and staff officer, he was very close to retirement. He was about 10 years older than the average age of those appointed to command other AIF brigades, and some of his fellow peacetime brigadiers had already been rejected as too old for the AIF. However, some contemporary records show him as 54, although it seems unlikely that someone as well known as Hughes could have falsified his age to get into the AIF.

At home Hughes had carried his age well, but the responsibilities of command, when added to the arduous and unhealthy conditions, proved too much for him on Gallipoli. Despite being relieved of his command following illness, he was determined to continue serving and, although he was no longer required at the front, he eventually obtained a posting to the Sea Transport Service, assisting with the movement of troops overseas during the later months of the war.

Shortly after the war Hughes retired from the army with the honorary rank of major general. For his active service he had been appointed a Commander of the Order of the Bath (CB), and was mentioned in despatches. But he remained haunted by the realisation that the one battle which was to be the climax of his long military life had been a disaster. He felt that circumstances had been cruel to him, and was angered by any suggestion that he had been responsible for what had happened at The Nek.

Frederic Godfrey Hughes was born at Windsor, a suburb of Melbourne, on 26 January 1858. His parents had migrated to Australia separately; his father, Charles, in 1836 and his mother, Ellen, in 1850. Charles Hughes had established properties in New South Wales and Victoria and had met Ellen during a visit to Britain. She followed him back to Victoria, where they were married. Bad luck and financial misfortune, then her husband's early death, caused Ellen to leave the land and take her family of three boys to Melbourne. An independent and capable woman, she was the dominant influence on Frederic's early life and lived to become the matriarch of a remarkable family. She guided her sons into their careers, and they became prominent in business, the army, sport, the church and medicine.

Frederic attended Melbourne Church of England Grammar School, then joined a leading land valuer and agent, before leaving in 1884 to set up on his own. He was tall, fair, and athletic. Both he and his brothers became well-known sportsmen. Frederic was an intercolonial rower and a foundation member of the Essendon Football Club and was a Victorian representative in the 1880 and 1881 seasons, retaining an active interest in sports throughout his life.[1] Meanwhile all three boys were brought up according to their mother's high church Anglican beliefs, and one, Ernest, duly became the leader of the Anglo-Catholic faction of the Church of England in Australia.

In 1875, aged 17 years, Frederic commenced his part-time military career, when he joined the St Kilda Artillery Battery as a driver. This popular and colourful city unit was commanded by Major (later Sir) Frederick Sargood, a wealthy businessman and conservative politician. In uniform, each of the men wore the letters 'SK' for St Kilda on their shoulders and they were irreverently known locally as 'Sargood's Kids'. Under Sargood's command, it was reputed to be the 'crack' battery of the time, and also 'the best dressed'.[2]

Sargood ran his unit as a precision team, concentrating on appearance, drill and competitive shooting. Hughes enjoyed the life and made a good impression. But promotion was slow: he was a sergeant in 1883 and was not commissioned until the following year. Later he would serve with Sargood on the committee of the influential Victorian Naval and Military Club. The connection no doubt served Hughes's military career well when, after 1883, for a number of terms, Sargood became Minister for Defence in the Victorian Government.

Frederic's marriage introduced him into Victoria's high society. On 1 October 1885 he wed Agnes Eva Snodgrass, the daughter of Peter Snod-grass, a sometimes hot-headed member of the Victorian Legislative Council and a protector of the interests of the large landowners. Her grandfather was Lieutenant Colonel Kenneth Snodgrass, a distinguished soldier and prominent early colonist. The couple had known each other since they were children, when both families were neighbours in the Seymour district. Frederic would later boast that his father and his wife's father 'were of the party who crossed over the borders to Port Phillip, with stock, in the year 1846'.[3]

Agnes Hughes was a little older than her husband and, like her mother-in-law, was a woman of intelligence and independent thought and action. In 1904 she became a founder of the conservative Australian Women's National League and in 1909 was elected state president. When Frederic joined the AIF in 1914, Agnes was presiding over an organisation she had built from 120 to 420 branches, with over 50,000 members. During the war she encouraged members to undertake patriotic and charitable work while, from 1916, she vigorously advocated the introduction of conscription.[4] She was also the sister of Janet, Lady Clarke, and this provided Frederic with immediate entry into the influential Clarke family circle.

Sir William Clarke was one of the richest men in the colony, having inherited vast Victorian rural holdings from his pioneering father, W.J.T. 'Big' Clarke. His first wife, Mary, had borne him four children, including his eldest son, Rupert, before her untimely death in a carriage accident. In 1873 he married the children's governess, Janet Snodgrass, and they had a further seven children. The Clarkes took up residence on their property surrounding Sunbury, 40 kilometres from Melbourne, and here in 1876 Sir William completed 'Rupertswood', his mansion named after his son and heir.

Sir William had an interest in military matters – he had served in the old Victorian Yeomanry for a while – and was actively concerned for the defence of the colony in which he had such an obvious stake. He gave money for military prizes, allowed part of his property to be used for camps and, in 1884, undertook to meet some of the expenses of a local volunteer corps. The government acceded to his proposal for a corps and provided a few ten-barrel machine-guns mounted on light carriages, and Clarke maintained the horses. It was called the Victorian Nordenfeldt Battery and was to operate as the guns for the Victorian cavalry. Several of Clarke's employees were among those who joined.

Through his connection with the Clarkes, Hughes obtained command of the unit. Originally, it had been intended that it be given to Rupert Clarke, a discontented and restless young man, in an attempt to interest and occupy him. The idea was not a success. Rupert's probationary appointment had to be extended and then, in 1886, he took leave to go to London. So close was Sir William's involvement in the corps that it was considered appropriate that his son's place be taken by someone else from within the family circle.[5]

Frederic's part-time military career had been solid but unspectacular to this point; he had served for nine years before receiving his first commission at the age of 26, and at 30 was still a lieutenant. Rupert's departure enabled him to transfer to the Nordenfeldt Battery and to take temporary charge of it. When it became obvious that young Rupert did not share his father's enthusiasm for the corps, Frederic's appointment was confirmed and on 20 August 1888 he was promoted to the rank of captain. This set the course of his military career for the next decade, and brought him into some prominence while extending his circle of social and military contacts.

Frederic Hughes' influence was further expanded when Andrew Chirnside, the squire of Werribee Park, offered to support a corps of horse artillery, with his son, Percy, in command. The government decided to amalgamate the contributions of the two families into a regiment designated the Victorian Horse Artillery, with Hughes as commanding officer. The change also saw an expansion of the Rupertswood half battery with the inclusion of several men from the city. Most were young professionals and the sons of some of Sir William's acquaintances. Such was the prestige of the Victorian Horse Artillery that several of these men chose to serve in its ranks, when they could have obtained commissions in other units.

The horse artillery became one of Victoria's showpieces, being only second to the Victorian cavalry in the order of precedence, and when on parade it took the right of the line. The Nordenfeldt guns had been replaced with four Armstrong artillery pieces, instructors were brought out from Britain, and elaborate uniforms copied from the Royal Horse Artillery were adopted. In command, Hughes looked splendid in a tight-waisted blue uniform almost dripping with gold braid and lace; he wore high polished boots, a white helmet, and was mounted on the best horse the Clarkes could provide. In 1891 he was promoted to major.

In the nineteenth century, patriotism may have been one motive for young men to join military units, but handsome uniforms, companionship and sporting and social activities were probably stronger inducements. Sports, military balls, camps and shooting competitions were important features of the part-time soldiers' calendars, particularly in exclusive units such as the horse artillery. Even its city men could match it on horseback with those off the properties, although the two did not mix socially.

The Chirnsides' connection with the regiment ended in 1893, when Percy's brother, George, who had become heir to Werribee Park, withdrew his support. Percy transferred to the Reserve of Officers, and never forgave his brother for disbanding the half battery.

The regiment was too dependent upon private support and interest to last for long. The aged Armstrong guns had caused problems in the past, but they had now deteriorated to the point of becoming a joke. They still looked fine draped with flowers in the Clarke's ballroom during special events, but they had outlived their usefulness in the field. While Hughes was always able to present and lead an outstanding competition outfit, with this equipment the horse artillery could not be seriously regarded as a fighting unit.

In 1893 Hughes took a tournament team to England. The tour, during which he was presented to Queen Victoria on four occasions, was a high-light of his military career.[6] Sir William Clarke provided the support for the detachment to participate in the annual military tournament at Islington and competitions at Bisley. The squad included members from Rupertswood and a few of the city men.

In 1897 the unit went into camp and had to undertake a light cavalry role, because the guns were no longer of any use. The government appeared to have lost interest and ignored appeals for support. The final blow came when Sir William died only a month later. The horse artillery did not last much longer. Victoria was in the grip of a long and savage economic depression, which had the government looking for all possible defence savings, and

Rupert Clarke was not prepared to maintain the financial support his father had given. Finally, the half battery was formally disbanded from 30 June 1897.

Hughes's military involvement, while it occupied a lot of his attention and provided useful contacts, was only part-time. Hughes was an energetic and industrious man, who succeeded in business and was vitally involved in local affairs. Within his family he was recalled fondly as 'kindly and solid'.[7] He cultivated a wide range of interesting and influential friends and continued to achieve military promotions. Following the disbandment of the horse artillery he transferred to the field artillery and soon afterwards became a staff officer on the Victorian Militia headquarters. In 1900 he was promoted to lieutenant colonel.

Frederic Hughes was an active and gregarious fellow. He was a man's man who mixed easily and enjoyed a range of masculine interests. In middle age he remained physically impressive. Although not considered an intellectual, he was 'an alert, articulate, observant and sometimes irascible man [who] mixed urbanity and geniality with toughness and shrewdness'.[8]

Hughes took no part in the South African War; family legend states that he was prevented from going because he was married and had a family. It is said to have been 'the big disappointment in his life'.[9] Yet it seems that he could probably have gone if he had wanted to, as other married officers had already been accepted. Still there was not much call for colonial officers of his relatively high rank. It is possible his services were not sought, simply because there was no need for them.

In 1903, as a consequence of Federation, the former colonial mounted units were reorganised as regiments of light horse. Hughes, in a departure from his former artillery associations, was given command of the 11th Australian Light Horse, a regiment which had been raised from the old Victorian Mounted Rifles, with its headquarters at Warrnambool in the state's Western District. Four years later he was promoted to colonel and made commander of the 4th Australian Light Horse Brigade. In 1912 he was placed in command of the 7th Light Horse Brigade, although this was more a change in nomenclature than organisation.

Although he was now a senior officer, Hughes had no war experience and much of his background lay in exclusive units better prepared for the tournament arena than the battlefield. His was the type of mind attracted by the pomp and prestige provided in this work. One of his officers wrote critically some time later: 'In time of war, as in peace, our brigadier's idea of soldiering was to salute smartly, roll a greatcoat correctly, and note the march discipline.'[10] If it was so, then it is not surprising that one of the few surviving records of the 11th Light Horse should reflect this. Following the regiment's camp at Langwarrin in 1906, Hughes had submitted a report in which he concentrated on the need to improve marching and saluting, 'in order to maintain the prestige of the regiment.'[11]

The military connections with the Clarkes had been retained when Reginald Clarke, Sir William's youngest son, also transferred to the 11th Light Horse Regiment. He was appointed adjutant over the heads of some other officers and, when Hughes was given the command of a brigade, Clarke followed him and was appointed his brigade major.

Hughes was also active beyond his business and military spheres and was prominent in civic affairs. When the war commenced he was living in 'Kantaka' on Alma Road, St Kilda. He had a long involvement with the suburb, and in 1898 had been elected a local councillor. He served on the council for 24 years, including two spells as mayor, in 1900–01 and again in 1911–12. The city's history recorded that '[he] gave to St Kilda of his best, and his name is one to be inscribed upon the list of the distinguished civic fathers'.[12] When he was accepted for the AIF, he did not foresee a long war and initially obtained 12 months' leave from the council. His occupation was then shown as company manager and sharebroker.

Among his business interests, Hughes was director of the Dunlop Rubber Company of Australasia Ltd, and before he embarked he was guest of honour at a smoke night arranged by the company. The general manager presented him with an illuminated address and a pair of binoculars; in proposing a toast, he declared that it was 'men of the calibre of Colonel Hughes who assisted in keeping the British Empire in its proper position.'[13] There were several other farewells, and more gifts, including some which may have been more appropriate for a senior officer at Waterloo but would be of little comfort on Gallipoli. The mayor presented a silver campaigning bottle on behalf of the council, and the members of the St Kilda Tradesmen's Club gave a silver cigar case and matchbox.

Had circumstances been different, Hughes would probably have sought Reginald Clarke as his brigade major for his AIF command, but Clarke had taken ill while he was in militia camp and died in hospital on 17 March 1914. A South Australian-born permanent officer, Percy Muir McFarlane, began his association with Hughes when he was appointed Clarke's replacement. Eventually, it was he who accompanied Hughes over to the AIF brigade, not as brigade major but in the more junior position as staff captain.

McFarlane made an important contribution to the new brigade during its formative months. He had a long career in the Australian army, beginning as a trooper in South Africa in 1900 with the 4th South Australian Imperial Bushmen's Contingent, and ending in 1940 when he retired with the rank of brigadier. After obtaining a commission in the South African Constabulary, he had commanded a troop in the former Boer territories for some years after the South African War. When he returned to Australia he joined the light horse, then in 1910 transferred to the Administrative and Instructional Staff of the Commonwealth's permanent forces. He was self-confident, active and hard-working, although his experience was described as having been gained more in the office than in the field. His nickname –'Tin Tacks' – was evidently derived from what a superior saw as 'his anxiety to get to the bottom of things'.[14]

Hughes appears to have had little say in the appointment of his brigade major. Such appointments were usually reserved for trained professionals. He had already worked with McFarlane, his staff captain, but it is likely that he only knew his new brigade major, Lieutenant Colonel Jack Antill, by reputation, if at all.

CHAPTER 4

The Brigade Major

Lieutenant Colonel John Macquarie Antill, the brigade major of the 3rd Light horse Brigade, was a 48-year-old professional soldier who had a long association with the old mounted rifles and the light horse regiments in New South Wales. Together, he and Hughes would become central characters in the controversy which arose following the battle at The Nek. It is important to trace the backgrounds of these two men in order to throw some light on their relationship and their conduct in battle.

Jack Antill was descended from a distinguished line of British army officers, from whom he inherited an interest in history and a sense of his own destiny. He was born on 26 January 1866 at 'Jarvisfield', a property at Picton, New South Wales, originally established by his grandfather, in the large comfortable house his father had built only a year or so earlier.

It must have seemed unusual that in the 3rd Light Horse Brigade, composed as it was of Victorians, South Australians and Western Australians, such a senior position should have been given to an officer so closely connected to New South Wales. Antill's family had deep roots in the state. His grandfather, Major Henry Colden Antill, had served in America and India before coming to the colony, where he was the devoted aide-de-camp to Governor Lachlan Macquarie. The major was one of the prominent citizens in the early settlement and was duly granted a tract of land, which he named 'Jarvisfield' in honour of the governor's own estate in Scotland. A private village was developed on the property, which grew to be called Picton. The picturesque little town, to which Jack Antill regularly returned, lay nestled in the hills on the main southern road from Sydney. The railway arrived early, providing a speedy and reliable link to the city.

It was often said that Jack Antill was born to be a soldier. In reality, the career was probably chosen by his father, who had decided that his eldest son, Robert Henry, would inherit 'Jarvisfield'. Young Jack was a good sportsman interested in boxing and fencing and was an experienced horse rider. Clearly he was robust enough to pursue a career in the field in which his family had been long involved. He received his first taste of military life as a cadet at Sydney Grammar School, and in 1887 he joined the local reserves.

In 1889 a mounted company was raised at Picton under the patronage of the Antills, and Jack was given the command. The arrangement had obvious parallels with the Clarkes' involvement in the Nordenfeldt Battery in Victoria, although here the Antills' contribution was not so closely defined. The company became part of the New South Wales Mounted Infantry Regiment under Captain Henry Beauchamp Lassetter.

The mounted infantry had initially been formed to provide a permanent cadre of mounted troops for the New South Wales defence forces. It had been decided to expand the unit to a full regiment by the inclusion of part-time country companies, each of three officers and 47 rank and file. In 1890 the permanent company was disbanded, and three years later the regiment was renamed the New South Wales Mounted Rifles.

The family's connection with the mounted rifles became even stronger after the commanding officer married the youngest of the Antill girls in August 1891. Harry Lassetter had been born in Sydney, where his family ran one of the largest and best known city stores, but had received his education in England, after which he entered Sandhurst Royal Military College. He obtained his commission in 1880 and saw active service in Egypt and the Sudan with the South Staffordshire Regiment, before coming home to Australia.

Through the influence of his father, and possibly supported by his brother-in-law, Antill was brought to the attention of Major General Edward Hutton, then commanding the forces of the colony. Hutton arranged for him to be sent to India in 1893 to gain experience in the field with the British army. Upon his return in the following year, Antill was transferred to the permanent forces, retaining the rank of captain. He resumed his involvement with the mounted rifles as the regiment's adjutant.

Hutton was an important British military figure and a person of wide influence. He later served a second period in Australia, returning in 1902 and remaining for three years to undertake the organisation of the new Commonwealth army. With more efficiency than tact, he set about converting the old colonial units into a new citizens' force. This included the creation of the Australian Light Horse from the former various mounted regiments. Antill retained his association with Hutton, and even after the general retired home to England they continued to exchange letters.

It was the war in South Africa which established Antill's military reputation. He had the professional good fortune to hold a position in a regiment that would be required to play an important role in the war. Added to this, he had arrived at the front in time to take part in some of the most famous battles.

Antill was placed in command of a service squadron from his regiment, which was a part of the first contingent sent to the war from the Australian colonies. His unit – A Squadron, New South Wales Mounted Rifles – arrived at Capetown on 6 December 1899. He was present at the relief of Kimberley, the battles of Paardeberg and Osfontein, the entry into Bloemfontein, and the capture of Pretoria. At Paardeberg the mounted rifles assisted in locating the main Boer force under General Piet Cronje, which had tried to slip past the advancing British army. The British converged on the Boers, who were surrounded; with diminishing food supplies, their horses and stock killed, and having no doctors to attend their sick and wounded, they surrendered.

The capture of Cronje's army was the first major British victory of the war, and Antill's little band played a minor but quite recognisable part. In acknowledgment of its work, the squadron was given the honour of being among the first troops to enter the enemy's lines. Antill reported: 'We were first into the laager (which was a pit of dead and filth) to collect prisoners, wounded, arms, and ammunition, and it was a nauseous job.'[1] Later he sent Cronje's white surrender flag back to his brother at 'Jarvisfield'; it became a major attraction in Sydney when it was placed on display in the window of Lassetter's George Street store.

Further mounted rifles squadrons arrived from Australia and on 5 March 1900, at Osfontein, they combined to form a regiment, with Antill retaining command of A Squadron. When the regiment marched out of Bloemfontein, it became part of a strong brigade under Major General Edward Hutton, the same officer who had been commandant in New South Wales some years earlier. Hutton was an exponent of mounted warfare, and Antill once again impressed him. Within a few days he was mentioned by Hutton in a letter to the premier of New South Wales as having contributed to the successful work of the mounted rifles in an action at Vet River.

Later, in the fighting around Pretoria, Antill was again recognised with special praise. Following the actions leading up to the fall of this Boer capital, and in the battle which followed at Diamond Hill, Colonel H.B. de Lisle[2] reported:

> Major J.M. Antill, NSW Mounted Rifles, commanded this splendid Regiment for a considerable time during the absence of the Commanding Officer. On two occasions he led his Regiment at a gallop against positions held by the enemy. Proving himself to be a fearless and valuable leader in the field. He has shown great capacity in command of his regiment.[3]

Antill arrived back in Sydney on 8 January 1901. He had become something of a minor celebrity and his photograph appeared in most of the local publications on the war; he even received mention in the *Illustrated London News*. His experience contrasted with that of his brother Edward, who had gone to the war with A Battery of the New South Wales Artillery. Edward had a frustrating time chasing after the Boers and never really catching up with them.

Jack Antill did not stay at home for long. In March he left again for South Africa, this time as second-in-command of the 2nd New South Wales Mounted Rifles, a large regiment commanded by his brother-in-law. Although no more big battles were fought, the regiment saw a lot of service in the Transvaal during the guerrilla phase of the war. This time he was away for less than six months.

On 24 October 1901, in historic St James Church, Antill married Agnes Marion Willsallen in what the *Sydney Morning Herald* described as 'a fashionable wedding'. The couple had become engaged while he was at home between his tours of service in South Africa.

Jack Antill was by then established as an experienced and bold professional soldier. He had twice been mentioned in despatches, been appointed a Commander of the Order of the Bath (CB), and granted the brevet rank of lieutenant colonel for his war service. This last honour entitled him to the badges and privileges of a lieutenant colonel but not the pay or seniority. His service medal, worn after his CB, bore seven bars with the names of the battles in which he had taken part. It was something scarcely matched by any other local officer.

When his fighting expeditions were over, and now a married man, he returned to his regiment as adjutant, just as it was preparing to be split and converted into two regiments of light horse under the Commonwealth organisation. His duties were then considerably expanded by his appointment as chief instructor of light horse for the state. Possibly Hutton's hand was again at work. In 1904–06 he proudly emulated his grandfather by being appointed an aide-de-camp to the governor-general, Lord Northcote. In 1906, with the substantive rank of major and having turned 40, he retired from the army and went back to Picton, before later residing on a property owned by his in-laws at Gunnedah.

Five years later, in 1911, Antill was given the opportunity to return to soldiering, and he willingly took it. The Australian army was undergoing drastic changes and expansion resulting from the introduction of universal training. The scheme required that all young males undergo compulsory military service in the cadet forces and the militia. Additional officers and NCOs, particularly instructors, were required for the expanded force. Antill returned to the Administrative and Instructional Staff, a body of professional experienced soldiers, with his former rank and was appointed commandant of the Instructional Staff Schools. He assembled a small team of experienced officers and warrant officers to provide training at Albury, in southern New South Wales, for the army's permanent instructors.

Antill, who now became known to a new generation of young soldiers, already had the reputation of being a disciplinarian. His square stance, thrusting jaw, loud voice and narrowed eyes were intimidating. In South Africa Brigadier General Edwin Alderson,[4] commanding the mounted infantry, had said that 'his Contingent has been more under control and in hand than any of the Colonial troops I have seen'.[5] His seniors knew him to be tough and uncompromising. Brigadier General Joseph Gordon, commandant in New South Wales, had described him in 1906 as 'always a man to a man'.[6] But he was more than that – he was a rigid authoritarian. He believed that he applied discipline in his own behaviour and demanded it in others, and it showed in his demeanour. *Melbourne Punch* gave a colourful description of him:

When he instructs, he flails the instruction into his pupils with his tongue. Some officers to whom he tells the raw, uncloaked truth about themselves are apt to become offended. It is unfortunate, but to divorce Antill from his own particular manner would be to rob him of his effectiveness. Few men of his age could live long with him in a set-to. He is of the hard-hitting, finish-early school – a dangerous man to face. [He] can ride to a standstill the worst of the buckjumpers, and loves to do it. He has the clear cut face, the close shut mouth and the hard eye of the determined man. When he speaks there is a decisive ring about his words, which are as few as possible. He is a soldier all through.[7]

He became widely known as 'Bull' Antill. The nickname is revealing for, while it is an apparent reference to his toughness, there were other connotations. "Bull" had its own military meaning – the word is said to have originated in the Australian army to describe the excessive attention to drill and spit and polish. In the 3rd Light Horse Brigade the nickname had a humorous association. A 9th Light Horse officer many years later recalled that, rather than 'Bull Antill', the name was pronounced 'Bullant hill'[8]. This is confirmed in the diary of Lieutenant Colonel Alexander White, who consistently refers to Antill as 'Bullant'.

A number of young men destined to hold commands during the war were trained by Antill. Sir Richard Williams, in his autobiography, recalls his time at Albury, where Antill questioned his entitlement to sit examinations. Once this was settled, he made sure that Williams, a former bank clerk who was not very familiar with horses, qualified at the riding test by insisting that he ride the 100-kilometre round journey to Beechworth and back. Sixty years later Williams still recalled his discomfort: 'The commandant then told me I must "heal in the saddle", in which he assisted by ordering me to take the horse to collect the mail twice a day. It seemed to take a long time but it worked.'[9]

In 1911 Antill became one of the first Australian officers to fly when he accepted a ride as an observer in a flimsy Bristol Boxkite being demonstrated at the Liverpool camp. He was 'amazed to see so many Light Horse squadrons operating over such a widespread an area'.[10] Eventually, it was Williams who was accepted to attend the newly formed Central Flying School in Victoria. He then served as an officer in the First World War, commanding No. 1 Squadron, Australian Flying Corps, and continued on to become chief of the air staff and 'the father of the RAAF'.

Antill's manner sometimes brought him into controversy. In 1911 he had been appointed to the army's inspection staff. He was required to attend militia training camps and submit reports to the inspector-general. The assessment he made of a one-week camp held by the 5th Brigade at Liverpool in November–December 1913 plunged him into trouble and became the lowest point in his peacetime career.

In his report, he condemned the lack of discipline, the control and proficiency of the officers, the supervision, filthy lines, poor rifle exercises, bad marching, dirty band instruments and the appearance of the men. He not only complained about the militia officers but also attacked the permanent staff as well. His comments on Major Laurence Molloy, the adjutant of the 14th Australian Infantry Regiment, seem to have been quite cruel, and were later described in an official enquiry as having been grossly unfair. Molloy had been a fellow officer with Antill in South Africa and, while perhaps not brilliant, was a solid old soldier. The report caused a storm. A court of inquiry was held to investigate the claims that Antill was harsh and tactless, and had intentionally persecuted certain officers. The inquiry concluded that parts of the report were indeed unjust, unfair, misleading, and not supported by evidence.

Attention turned to Antill. The Military Board decided that he should be called upon to show why his services should not be dispensed with. But this time the board had gone too far. Antill responded by questioning the qualifications of some members of the court, and sought to have the matter dealt with by court-martial. The inquiry only had the power to investigate the initial report and, on legal advice, it was decided not to proceed further. However, it was suggested that the matter be borne in mind in regard to Antill's future employment. It was felt that he was unsuitable as an inspector for the inspector-general and his transfer to another state was 'a matter for consideration'.[11]

Antill's severe attitude may have concealed his unsettled professional and private life. He had now held the same rank in the army for over a decade, and had seen several of his former peers, and some of his juniors, promoted over him. There was James Gordon Legge who, with Antill, had commanded a squadron of the mounted rifles in some of the important actions in South Africa, and whose career had run roughly parallel for a few years after the war. But by 1914, with the rank of colonel, he was appointed the chief of the general staff. There were other regular officers such as William Bridges, Brudenell White and Harry Chauvel who, like

Antill, had been favoured by General Hutton's interest and were now leading figures in the Australian army. To make matters worse, most of the militia officers with whom he had to deal had only a fraction of his knowledge and experience. Clearly his career had not fulfilled his earlier expectations. The truth was that, while he was an intelligent man, he was rigid in his thinking and did not possess the quickness of mind or the fertile brain of those whose promotions he coveted.

Antill disliked emotion and to all outsiders maintained a hard exterior. To his family he could display wit and charm, and as a raconteur 'never hesitated to make a good story better'[12]. Only those closest to him would ever know of his interest in gardening, and literature, and of his passion for the theatre. The other side of his character was briefly revealed in an incident on Gallipoli in which he came across Sergeant Otto Hewett, a member of his brigade, doing a landscape drawing. Knowing Antill's reputation, the soldier said he saw trouble looming and was not surprised when he was told to report to headquarters. He was relieved to find that the brigade major had admired his work and wanted him to do some panoramic sketches.[13] Hewett was given the opportunity to produce more drawings and some of these eventually appeared in *The Anzac Book*, a soldiers' publication devised and edited by Charles Bean on Gallipoli. The use of Hewitt as an artist predated the appointment of official war artists in later campaigns.

With men Antill was usually severe and uncompromising, but with women he could be passionate and foolish. He had married in 1901 despite opposition from both parties' families. The union, which produced two of his daughters, was not a success, ending in divorce in 1914. He was involved with other women and his 'love intrigue' with a young Sydney actress was described by Edmond Samuels in his autobiography. The writer was a Sydney pharmacist who shared Antill's interest in the theatre and was an officer in the militia when they met at Victoria Barracks in Sydney. Samuels once conveyed a message from the actress, an occasion he later recalled: 'I was aware that I was facing a man who had the nickname of "Bull Antill" on account of his severe military bearing and manner.' He eventually got to know Antill better: 'Despite his outward show of being a hard disciplinarian, he had many qualities I admired.'[14]

Antill's behaviour over the Liverpool camp incident had almost destroyed his career. It was a bleak period and it coincided with the collapse of his marriage. It is likely that the two events were connected. Antill and his wife had been spending increasingly lengthy periods of time apart. Marion was much younger, pretty rather than beautiful, lively, and from a wealthy family. She was not one to be bullied or cowered by his bluster. Finally, after a decade of married life, she declared that she was a young woman, was fond of life and excitement and preferred to live in the city.[15] In 1912 she took their eldest daughter, aged 10, and walked out; soon afterwards she went to live independently in London. Antill was flattened.

Marion refused her husband's pleas to return, and eventually, even as the Liverpool affair broke around him, he reluctantly began divorce proceedings: 'I was at a dead end and notwithstanding the odium of it all, the wretched publicity and all, no other course was open to me.'[16] Added to his military worries, he found the scandal over his divorce also affected how he was regarded within his social circles. Similar ugly tattle would visit him again a decade on when he was named a co-respondent in a widely reported Adelaide divorce case.

The controversy surrounding the Liverpool camp affair continued into 1914, and its shadow was still hanging heavily over Antill when the war began. His early reputation had been won as a fighting officer, and he now thrilled at the prospect of being rid of peacetime soldiering and going off to war again. With the forming of the AIF, he was soon 'straining every nerve to get away in some capacity'.[17]

In better times he might have hoped to be given a command. Instead, he was made enrolment officer for the AIF in Sydney, responsible for selecting the New South Wales men for the first contingent. The *Sydney Mail* published a short article on his duties, which was accompanied by a photograph of him that must have been at least 10 years old as it showed him still with a dark Victorian moustache. 'No one is better qualified than he for this important work,' it said. 'He can tell almost at a glance what a man is made of, and his long experience as a soldier is of immense value to him in making the selection of the men who are to represent Australia at the front.'[18] This proclaimed ability to be able to judge a man 'almost at a glance' should have come under some question after the Liverpool incident. Further doubt must have been created when a willing young volunteer of German-born parents was enlisted after Antill had opposed his being accepted.[19]

Eventually, as the AIF grew and more officers were needed, his experience could no longer be ignored. Antill's appointment to the 3rd Light Horse

Brigade had been decided by a selection committee. Although he was very senior for such a position, it may have been felt that this tough professional might cover up some deficiencies that Colonel Frederic Hughes' age might reveal. It also seems that the appointment to a brigade outside of Antill's home state was in line with the suggestion made by the Military Board that his transfer to another military district be considered.

Although he probably had no say in the matter of Antill's appointment, Hughes had no reason to be personally concerned. Whatever the brigade major's relations were with his subordinates, it seems that it was part of his authoritarian nature to serve his superiors well and to seek their approbation.

CHAPTER 5

Officers and Men

The commands of each of the brigade's three regiments were given to officers with previous long service in the militia. Lieutenant Colonels Albert Miell and Noel Brazier of the 9th and 10th Light Horse were both commanding militia regiments when they received their AIF appointments, while Alexander White of the 8th Regiment was a brigade major with a light horse brigade in Victoria. They had all been quick to offer their services soon after the war started. White might have been able to find a place in the first contingent, but his only child was born at the same time as his new appointment, so he was held back and engaged in staff work at Victoria Barracks to allow him to organise his family affairs. Brazier and Miell were 48 and 44 years old respectively, and Miell was a veteran of the South African War. White was considerably younger, aged 32.

Alexander Henry White had been born in Ballarat and in civilian life had recently taken up a position in the family business of Joe White and Co. Pty Ltd, Foster Maltings at Collingwood, Melbourne. He was the third son in his family and the company was the main provider of malt to most of Australia's leading breweries.[1] He began his military service as a private in the Victorian Mounted Rifles and received his first commission in 1904, in the light horse. After seven years he was promoted to captain. Early in 1914 he rose another rank and was made brigade major of the 5th Light Horse Brigade. His transfer to the AIF brought with it promotion to lieutenant colonel and command of his own regiment. His wife later said that his 'whole heart and soul was in his military work from the time he joined the old Mounted Rifles in Ballarat after leaving school'.[2]

White was an astute, likeable and popular officer. Both his superiors and those under his command respected him, while his letters to his wife reveal him to have been a gentle and decent man. He took with him to the war a

Bible in which he had placed a newspaper clipping titled "A Creed", part of which said:

> Let me be a little braver
> When temptation bids me waver,
> Let me strive a little harder
> To be all that I should be.
> Let me be a little meeker
> With the brother that is weaker
> Let me think more of my neighbour
> And a little less of me.[3]

As unlikely as these sentiments seem for someone about to go off to lead men in war, they may well have expressed White's personal creed.

In an interview in 1984, Jack Dean recalled his old commanding officer: 'A wonderful man: an officer and a gentleman. He was popular throughout the regiment. Everybody would have followed him anywhere.'[4] Lionel Simpson, who saw White wounded on Gallipoli and was among the casualties when White was killed, agreed that he was 'a good man'.[5] Fellow officers spoke of him as 'very keen and energetic'.[6]

Comradeship and the possibility of adventure in far off places blended with White's idealism. Only after he left his home did he begin to discover a conflict between his new military obligations and those to the young family he left behind.

Brazier of the 10th Regiment was perhaps a more complex character. He had been born in Victoria, the son of a clergyman. His mother had died young, so he was largely brought up by an elder sister. He began working in a newspaper office but by hard study managed to qualify as a surveyor. This profession was in demand when he arrived in Western Australia and soon he was able to afford to take up a property he called 'Capeldene', at Kirup. He was attracted to the place because the hills reminded him of the Gippsland district of Victoria. Although not a particularly good farmer, he did have a strong interest in horses and a good eye for them.

In the decade before the war Brazier had purchased the champion trotter, General Tracey, from New Zealand. The arrival of his famous stallion marked Brazier as a notable breeder and contributed to the improvement of the blood lines in Western Australia.[7] This involvement with horses may have led Brazier into the light horse. The mount he took to war was named General Panic, a six-year-old son of the famous sire. It was regarded as the best horse of the light horse in the west.

Brazier had an interesting and unusual association with his second-in-command, Major Alan Love. Not long after Brazier was first commissioned in the local militia light horse the regiment had come under Love's command.[8] Major Love, a city accountant in civil life, retired a few years later, transferring to the Unattached List in January 1911. He came off the Retired List to join the AIF, this time to serve under Brazier, who had once been his junior. Some of the other officers in the 10th Regiment also knew both men from their own time in the militia.

Brazier worked hard to bring his regiment together, travelling through the state's settled regions to personally select men and horses. It eventually fought on Gallipoli and in the Sinai and Palestine campaigns, earning an impressive list of battle honours, which were passed to a later citizen force regiment that was re-numbered to perpetuate the deeds of the old 'Tenth'. The title of 'Father of the Regiment' has been conferred on him.[9]

Albert Miell was well known in pastoral, Masonic and business circles from Adelaide to Broken Hill, and was the most experienced of the three commanding officers. He could trace his military involvement back to 1888, when he joined the local forces, and by 1914 had risen to command of the 24th (Flinders) Light Horse. Illness had held him back from going to the South African War until 1901, when he served as a lieutenant in the 5th South Australian contingent. Like White and Brazier, Miell was married with a family. His son, Gordon, was old enough to enlist in the AIF in 1918 and served in Palestine in the regiment that had been raised under his father's command four years earlier.

Most of the brigade's officers also came from the militia. To the likes of Antill, the professional soldier, these were amateurs who would have to learn quickly. Where they were available, permanent soldiers from the Administrative and Instructional Staff were accepted to serve on the headquarters, or to stiffen the ranks of warrant officers and senior NCOs. There were also several officers who had recently graduated from the new Royal Military College at Duntroon, in what had been designated the future national capital.

The bearing and experienced military manner of the Duntroon officers belied the fact that these 20-year-olds were the youngest officers in their regiments. Three of them, Lieutenants Charles Dale, Leo Anderson and Charles Arblaster, had joined the 8th Light Horse in camp during November. Another Duntroon boy, Horace Robertson, was posted to the 10th Regiment. Dale and Anderson were to die at The Nek, while young Arblaster would go on to be a hero of the attack at Fromelles in France the following year and die of wounds received there. Robertson survived the war and eventually retired from the army after a lifetime of active and colourful service, during which he became famously known as 'Red Robbie', with the rank of lieutenant general and a knighthood.

Anderson and Dale had joined the Royal Military College in March 1912, after having been in the Victorian cadets and, for a brief time, the militia. Dale was active and athletic and excelled at Australian Rules football. Anderson was more studious and won several study prizes at the college, including the Australian National Defence League's gold medal for the highest marks. Fair, and small in stature, he had difficulty concealing his youth. A friend who saw him on Gallipoli reported that 'little Anderson is trying to look the old trench soldier with a six-haired beard'.[10] Still, few who watched him doubted that he should one day be a general. The brigade's Duntroon officers had been granted their commissions after accelerated training to allow them to accompany the troops departing for the war.

Many of the men in the AIF's early ranks had had some experience under the compulsory military service scheme, a few had been in the British army, and there were some older men who had seen active service and displayed medal ribbons. The official historian estimated that three-quarters of the early light horse enlistments had some training, although this is not borne out by the experience of the 3rd Light Horse Brigade.[11] Men joining the light horse often came from areas well away from the drill halls and army depots and so had not been obliged to participate in the compulsory training scheme. The 9th Light Horse claimed that little more than one-third of the men first enlisted came from the militia and a similar figure seems to have been evident in the 10th Regiment.[12]

Some of those enlisting in the ranks had already made a mark in life. Gresley Harper was a 32-year-old solicitor and a respected professional man in Perth. He and his younger brother, Wilfred, who was a farmer, enlisted on the same day in A Squadron of the 10th Light Horse. Despite his university education, maturity, and friendship with the Brazier family, Gresley did not seek a commission and the brothers served together in the ranks. Nine members of the influential Perth City Club volunteered for the regiment; only three were accepted as officers.

Another from the legal profession was Mervyn Higgins. A strong and good-looking young man, he came from one of Victoria's distinguished and privileged, if sometimes controversial, families. His father was Justice Henry Bourne Higgins, who, while a member of parliament, had opposed the sending of troops to the South African War as unnecessary and unjust. In 1906 he was appointed a judge of the High Court of Australia and is remembered for his landmark Harvester Judgement, in which he set a minimum wage for unskilled workers.

Mervyn Higgins was not as intellectual as his father, but he was regarded as quiet, personable and athletic. He was an only child and the focus of loving parents. At school he had been called 'Frenchy' because of the superior French accent he had acquired from his governess. At university he was 'Buggins'. A friend fondly described him:

A cow's lick and a happy grin
Broad shoulders and large feet,
A sunburned nose and stubborn chin.
And Mervyn is complete.[13]

He attended Oxford, where he was remembered more as a sportsman than a scholar; the Oxford Eight beat Cambridge in 1910 with Higgins in the crew. He came home in 1912 and was a barrister when the war began. His father, who was in London, received a cable: 'Anxious volunteer service. Uncle John willing manage your affairs if you are agreeable.'[14] He had had some military training in Britain and was an enthusiastic soldier. He joined the 8th Light Horse as a lieutenant shortly before the regiment left Australia.

Higgins was socially far removed from most of the light horse rank and file, among whom there were some 'hard cases'. Several of these enlisted in the heady early days of the war, but the dull routine of training and the restrictions of military discipline soon left them discontent. They simply left the camps and did not return. In 1914 it was still possible to fill these empty ranks and the efforts to locate deserters were often half-hearted.

Among those who stayed long enough to achieve an inglorious record was a driver in the 10th Light Horse. This troublesome soldier was court-martialled for insubordination on Gallipoli, a serious offence at the front.

He was sentenced to 35 days Field Punishment No. 1 and then sent to the Abassia detention barracks. This probably saved him from sharing the same fate as many of his mates. Eventually, he was diagnosed as suffering from venereal disease and ordered back to Australia, where the civil police awaited him. He was discharged in Perth, probably as glad to be rid of the army as it was to be of him.

There were also some men of mystery, such as London-born teenager Rollo Alban. The son of a former officer in the Indian army, he had entered the Royal Military College, Sandhurst, where he stayed for a year before being withdrawn. He had obtained sufficient examination marks but appears to have been failed for other unrecorded reasons.[15] He was sent out to Australia to try farming, although his occupation was shown as 'labourer' when he enlisted in the 8th Light Horse in October 1914. He had not been able to match the success of his elder brother, who also served in the war, was repeatedly decorated, and became a lieutenant colonel and a holder of the Distinguished Service Order with two bars. Young Rollo was killed at The Nek, aged 19, simply a trooper in an Australian regiment.

Men were enlisted between the ages of 18 and 35 years, although senior officers and some of the warrant officers and NCOs were often older. Soon the upper age limit was raised, allowing more South African War veterans to join without having to falsify their ages. The oldest man in the 8th Light Horse appears to have been Major James O'Brien, the second-in-command, at 52 years. His counterparts in the 9th and 10th Regiments, Carew Reynell and Alan Love, were 31 and 42 respectively. The average age of the officers in the 8th and 10th Regiments was 32.5 years. Among the other ranks, this average was 25.5 and 26.8 years.

The men came from a variety of backgrounds. In many respects the brigade was a representative gathering of Australian males. Noticeable variations from the national averages were the understandably very high proportion of unmarried men, and a higher number who claimed adherence to the Church of England. Not surprisingly, the membership was even more typical of the AIF overall. Even here the brigade had a higher proportion of single soldiers. More importantly, there was a demonstrably higher ratio of primary producers and men in rural employment. This was most pronounced in the 10th Light Horse.

All three regiments drew the majority of their members from the agricultural and primary producer groups, including more than half of those in the 10th Light Horse. In these regiments, the proportions are far in excess of both the national average (which was 25 per cent) and the various state averages. Similar occupations are noted in all regiments: pastoralists, farm labourers, farmhands, stockmen, jackeroos, horse-breakers and graziers. These are the occupations of men usually quite used to horses. At least one occupation – pearler – was possibly unique to the western state. The 8th Light Horse also drew heavily (30 per cent) on men working in the industrial sector.

The 10th Regiment had a higher proportion of unskilled single immigrant men on its roll. There was still a pioneering quality about life in the rural west. That, and the allure of the goldfields, had attracted migrants from overseas and interstate seeking work. British-born men were noticeable. More than one in every eight in the original regiment claimed as their next of kin a relative, usually a parent, living in the United Kingdom. Typically these men were in their early or mid-twenties.[16]

Although there were a couple of university-educated men in the ranks, the force was not as egalitarian as legend would have it, with most officers coming from the pastoral sector or the professions. Major Reynell noted that an officer in his regiment was a tradesman: 'Cook is a conscientious, well intentioned fellow with a good deal of common sense and energy but lacks the power of controlling others. His age – 44 – and his civil occupation have been heavily against him.'[17] Social position was not to count for so much on Gallipoli. Major Alfred Cook, the master butcher from Semaphore, South Australia, and veteran of the South African War, died in hospital from wounds received on 12 June 1915. The news of his death, it was reported, 'cast a gloom over the regiment, as he was respected and loved by all ranks'.[18]

Although it was said that the light horsemen generally were not highly motivated in a religious sense, it is noticeable that very few in the brigade declined to state adherence to an organised religion.[19] There may have been a tendency for some men to say that they were Church of England simply because it was the largest, and therefore the most acceptable, religious group in Australia. Membership of an organised church in 1915 could be an indication of national origin (as in the strong Irish-Catholic population), social status or even political beliefs. The 8th Light Horse showed a remarkably high proportion (26 per cent) of Presbyterians, which included the commanding officer. All the three regiments had low numbers of Roman Catholics.

While the 8th Light Horse was recruited from across the state, it always claimed a strong association with the Victorian Western District. In this region at least two-thirds of the pioneering settlers had been of Scottish origin and their descendants now joining the light horse had retained the Presbyterian faith.[20] While the number of Roman Catholics in the brigade was low, the proportion rose to 16 per cent among the private soldiers. The working-class Irish were more likely to be city men seeking to join the infantry.

In the first year of the war, the overwhelming majority of men enlisting were single. There was an obvious reluctance by married men to leave their families and their jobs. Even among the officers, who tended to be older, there were many who were single. In the 8th Regiment only about one-third of the officers were married. While married men tended to delay their enlistment, some of the single men who had joined up took the opportunity to wed before they went overseas. At least four of the officers who were destined to die at The Nek were married shortly before the brigade sailed: Charles Dale, Edward Henty, Thomas Redford and Vernon Piesse. Dale's young wife was in the first weeks of her pregnancy when he departed.

Lieutenant Ted Henty personified the Victorian Western District's contribution to the 8th Light Horse. He was the grandson of Stephen Henty who, with his pioneering brother, belonged to the first European family to settle in Victoria. Henty lived all his short life around Hamilton. He was the leader of the district's pre-war light horse troop and this was described as 'his only hobby'. He commanded a mounted guard for the first departing local volunteers not long before he, 'with a sort of enthusiastic pleasure', also enlisted. Before leaving he was married in the same church in which he had been baptised and confirmed.[21]

Some men were able to use their civilian trades and special skills in the army. A brigade needed its own saddlers, shoeing-smiths and farriers, so blacksmiths and others employed in these trades made an easy transition. There was a financial bonus as well, because most of these were paid an extra shilling per day. Some cooks found that their former occupation was now their rank, and there were some telegraph operators who quickly became signallers.

Some of the transitions were not so easily explained. There were instances where a baker became a trumpeter, a hairdresser became a sergeant, a clergyman was now a troop corporal, and one officer's batman had previously been a teamster. But the majority of men, whatever their civilian callings, were now 'private' soldiers (although it has been said that anything less private is hard to imagine). From April 1915 the light horse privates were called 'troopers'.

After embarkation a private was paid six shillings each day; one shilling was deferred until the termination of his service. Married men were told they must sign over at least two-fifths of their money to their wives, and three-fifths if there were children. Spouses also became entitled to a separation allowance. Pay increased with rank. For example, a lieutenant colonel received £1 17s 6d per day, and a lieutenant 17s 6d.

The pay rates were generous by soldiers' standards of the day. Once overseas, the Australians soon gained a reputation as free-spenders and were quickly targets for touts and vendors. In comparison, the British soldier was still tied to the old 'King's shilling'. The AIF pay reflected the pre-war belief that members of a citizen army should receive fair pay for a day's work. In many respects the armies were quite different in social attitudes and there were some penalties and restrictions on the British soldier which did not exist for the Australians. Certain characteristics attributed to the AIF had been carried over from peacetime.

It was not possible to assemble the whole brigade before its departure for overseas, so Hughes and Antill had to travel in order to meet the officers and inspect the regiments. Jack Dean remembered his unit's first view of Antill at Broadmeadows. 'He had a reputation as a fire-eater. A big fierce-looking joker,' he recalled.[22]

The two officers made the journey to Western Australia separately. Hughes was there first for a few days in October 1914, and inspected Brazier's regiment, reporting on his return that he could only express his admiration for the troops there. 'Very hardy and tough,' he said. 'They were men who had resided in the country, and who knew how to put up with rough usage.'[23] Antill met Brazier for the first time in early January and inspected the regiment.

Antill's visit to the 9th Light Horse in November at Morphettville, South Australia, before it had moved to Broadmeadows, had not gone so smoothly. The officers and NCOs had received one of his notorious tongue-lashings. He was apparently unbowed by the reaction to the trouble he had caused at Liverpool camp 18 months earlier. Antill made no concessions for these men who were still very aware that they had offered their services voluntarily. His remarks were 'resented by every man in camp … [and] the officers had the greatest difficulty in keeping the men in hand.'[24] Next morning the NCOs paraded before Lieutenant Colonel Miell and asked to be discharged. The officers also placed their protests before him. The situation could have quickly become ugly, but somehow Miell was able to bring things under control, and no more seems to have been said about it.[25] A local newspaper reporter tried to obtain a statement from Antill at the railway station as he was preparing to go back to Melbourne. This time he was more tactful. He would only say that 'the troops are a fine type of men'.[26]

It may have been the trouble in South Australia, or possibly some similar incidents at Broadmeadows, that caused the *Melbourne Punch* to report in February: 'Everybody does not like the Antill manner when he is met for the first time as a trained capable man instructing others whom he at least regards as untrained and incapable.' Seemingly unaware of the Liverpool uproar, the report added: 'In New South Wales nobody minds it. They are used to it. In other states … Antill's tongue comes as a new discovery.'[27]

By January 1915 all ranks were becoming impatient to leave the austere training camps and dull routine to get off to the war. Late in the month the two regiments at Broadmeadows were able to farewell Melbourne by marching fully equipped on horseback through the city. Officers and men rose early and rode to the Haymarket, where horses were fed, watered and briefly rested. Then they set off in column of route. Crowds assembled for more than half an hour in front of Parliament House where the governor-general took up his position to receive the salute.

A parade of hundreds of mounted men stretching the entire length of the city blocks, with horses' hoofs clattering on the roadway, marching behind their band, also mounted, was a thrilling sight. As the clocks struck midday the long noisy column turned from Collins Street into Spring Street. There were cries of 'Here they are!', and the excited crowds pressed forward, cheering.

Colonel Hughes's old heart must have nearly burst with pride as he led his brigade up to the saluting base. Following him was Antill, then came the band, with White and his regiment. Miell was next, leading the 9th Light Horse, then the brigade train, signallers, and ambulance. The *Herald* reported that the men appeared to be a better physical type than previous parades and estimated that 80 per cent must be countrymen.[28]

'Simply magnificent', declared the governor-general. The brigade camped the night at Heidelberg before returning to Broadmeadows. A few days later the Western Australians held a parade for their Sunday visitors.

Not long after these final appearances the first troops boarded the transports to take them to Egypt. By the end of February 1915 the whole brigade had left its home shores.

CHAPTER 6

Egypt

When the troopships of the first AIF contingent had left Australia, they were in fear of armed naval raiders operating in the Indian Ocean and so sailed in convoy under a heavy naval escort. The German threat was real enough: HMAS *Sydney*, one of the accompanying warships, located and destroyed the raider SMS *Emden* in a one-sided encounter off the Cocos-Keeling Islands. It was a great victory for the infant Royal Australian Navy, and it meant that future troopships leaving from Australia could proceed with little fear of being molested. Consequently, the transports carrying the 3rd Light Horse Brigade left Melbourne and Fremantle independently, and for several weeks the brigade was strung out across the seas between Australia and Suez.

The 10th Light Horse was the first to depart. On 8 February 1915 two squadrons left Western Australia on the *Mashobra*. The remaining squadron, together with the first reinforcements, did not follow until the 17th. The departure for the war of the state's light horse was an event to celebrate. The two squadrons, with Brazier at their head, marched from Claremont to Fremantle and began loading horses. A huge crowd gathered to farewell them and the boisterous demonstration concealed the deep heartfelt concerns of many of the parents, wives, brothers and sisters. There were nervous laughs, hugs and tears before the men were all finally assembled on board the ship. The sound of a band playing the national anthem, wild waving and noisy cheers accompanied the ship as it slowly drew out from the wharf. Many of the families gathered there were to retain the fond memory of this scene as their last sight of loved ones.

In contrast to the Western Australians, the other troops left quietly without any dock-side farewells. Most of the 9th Regiment left from Melbourne on the *Karoo* and the *Armidale* on 11 February. While a few officers, some men and more than 100 horses had sailed early in the month, the main component of the 8th Light Horse, on a troopship bearing the appropriate name of *Star of Victoria*, did not depart until the 24th. These Victorians had been able to take some short leave a few days earlier to say their goodbyes. After loading, the *Star of Victoria* moved out and stood off Williamstown. Tom Austin, who had joined the AIF straight out of school, eventually became the regiment's adjutant and a chronicler of its war exploits. That evening he recalled that 'a few hours were spent leaning over the rails looking at the lights of Melbourne, and speculations of our future doings were many and varied'.[1] The ship got under way during the night and next morning the troops watched their coastline slip away over the stern. Austin continued:

> The world was now before us and though full of eagerness and glad to be on our way to the front many of us looked back on our Broadmeadows days with a sigh. The life there had taught us much, the Country man had got to know a good deal of the city, and the City man had grown to love the open air life and exercise of the camp. We had become wise in the many fine points of a soldier's life, such as fatigue dodging, orderly rooms etc. We knew the YMCA was the place to find a man when he was required for fatigue or guard, that the dirtiest man in the camp was the cook, and that night time was the time to make up all shortages in kit and saddlery and that the Quartermaster Sergeant was the best man to buy beer for.[2]

The ships were of varying size and vintage and moved at different speeds to Colombo, on to Aden, then Port Said, and disembarked their passengers at Suez or passed through the Suez Canal to Alexandria. As each crossed the equator, 'crossing the line' ceremonies were conducted, usually with some rough fun at the expense of a few of the officers. Brazier enthusiastically entered into the clowning and appeared dressed in a feather head-dress and a lot of red paint, to represent 'Chief Kirup of Kapeldene'. He wrote: '19th Feb. Crossed the line. Ceremony the funniest thing I ever saw. Much laughter.'[3]

As the Victorians neared Colombo, Colonel White addressed his thoughts to his wife: 'Lectured NCOs. Spoke to them very earnestly about swearing and gambling among the troops – also warned them about the native women. I am feeling splendid, the voyage so far … has been one long holiday and loaf, only wish I had you all with me.'[4]

The *Mashobra*, with the 10th Light Horse, was the first to reach Colombo and the men were allowed ashore under the supervision of the officers. Earlier Australian contingents had behaved wildly and a close watch was kept on these latest arrivals. Brazier observed that the Australians were unpopular with the locals. The 9th Light Horse was not so lucky. Only officers and some NCOs were allowed off the ships when they arrived.

Once ashore, Major Reynell heard of the Royal Navy's attempts to force the Dardanelles to shell Constantinople and put Turkey out of the war. He saw the prospect of quickly getting to the front: 'If these [operations] are successful it should relieve the necessity for a large garrison in Egypt and we may after a month in Egypt for conditioning horses be sent on to Europe or Constantinople.'[5] At Aden he sought more news. This time he heard false reports that the Australians were to be sent to Smyrna.

Carew Reynell had already impressed his personality on the brigade. He was 31 years old, having been born in South Australia, where his grandfather had established one of the state's earliest wineries. Reynell also became a winemaker and, from the age of 19, managed the family business and set about making the Reynella brand widely known.[6] He was one of those remarkable officers, some of whom became famous throughout the AIF, who went at everything head-on. Antill came to regard him as 'a splendid man [and] an exceptionally fine and dashing leader'.[7]

Antill held no similar feelings for Brazier, with whom he shared the sea voyage. The brigade major had been sent to Perth to accompany the Western Australians to Egypt and while aboard the *Mashobra* was Officer Commanding Troops. Trouble developed between the two men as soon as the ship left the wharf. Evidently the moment that the farewells were over, Antill addressed the troops, saying: 'This is the worst disciplined regiment I have ever seen.' Brazier, who was intensely proud of his command, was cut to the core. 'I did not say anything, but I felt a lot,' he later wrote.[8] Some other minor incidents followed, which any other person may have chosen to ignore. But it was not in Brazier's nature to let such matters pass and he was soon making his resentment clear. The antipathy which developed between them set the tone of their future relationship.

The ships carrying the three regiments reached Egypt over four weeks up to 4 April. As they approached Suez, the men became aware that they were entering a theatre of war. There were a number of dark and impressive warships to be seen, and on the *Star of Victoria* full ash bags were piled against the handrails as protection from any Turkish rifle fire. While moving through the Suez Canal, the men exchanged greetings with Indian troops manning the trenches along the vital waterway.

Colonel White was not enthusiastic about the prospects of being stuck in Egypt, training:

> I want to get right up to the front now. I want to fight and do my job well, and then come home. Sitting in the desert for months is no good at all; it's bad. Bad for discipline, bad for morale, bad for health. But still why do I growl; we are soldiers and must do what we are told. I sure do want to rush things, but all the same I do hope they won't break our hearts with delay. This regiment is trained, and well trained, they can leave that to me. I know when they are fit, and they are quite fit as soon as the horses carry us again.[9]

Almost a month went by, from the time that the squadrons began to arrive, before the whole brigade could be assembled. As each squadron landed, it was placed on a train for the six- or seven-hour journey to Cairo. From there the men led their horses out 15 kilometres to Mena camp, with baggage following on electric tramcars. The camp was already occupied by the 1st Australian Division and the light horsemen could see how fit and trained their countrymen had become. It was more than two weeks before the horses had sufficiently recovered from the sea voyage to be ridden, so for a while training was limited to the rifle range and dismounted drills.

Mervyn Higgins had not been able to say goodbye to his parents when he left Melbourne, because they had been in England. They were now travelling home, so they stopped off in Egypt and were already in Cairo when he arrived at Mena Camp. On his first free day the family went to church and next day travelled to Port Said. There, father and son walked together, expressing their feelings and concerns in soft words or simple silences. These were precious last moments which would have been envied by thousands of other parents in Australia. Theirs was the inescapable fear of all families, that they might never be together again.[10]

Although everyone was anxious to finish training and be sent to the front, the first few weeks at Mena were pleasant enough. Exercises in the desert were often arduous, but usually there was spare time in the afternoon and evenings and the Australians found plenty to entertain them. Trooper

McConnan reported: 'There are native shops all around the camp and these are quite like little townships. We can buy almost anything without going to Cairo and there are four picture theatres.'[11] The city was only a tram journey away and the men were drawn there for amusement. Many simply became tourists, while others found many ways of getting into trouble in a city where squalor stood beside opulence and vice beside piety. Colonel White had some pleasant off-duty moments with Hughes, Antill and other members of the staff. 'The old Brigadier and Bullant and Tintacks are all very decent,' he said. But he noticed that Hughes was finding the work hard-going, adding that 'the old chap I think is ageing a lot'.[12]

Hughes was reunited with two members of his family at Mena. His own son, Arthur, had come over earlier in the 4th Light Horse, which he had joined as a private the previous September, and his brother's son was an infantry sergeant in the 7th Battalion. While in Egypt Hughes arranged for this nephew, Wilfrid Kent Hughes, to be commissioned and transferred to his headquarters. Later, on Gallipoli in August, his son was also commissioned and transferred across.

Hughes had accepted and extended patronage in many of his affairs. The appointments of both his nephew and his son to staff positions were straightforward cases of nepotism, although both young men would finish the war with fine records. Nineteen-year old Kent Hughes wrote to his parents: 'I am now Uncle Fred's orderly officer (or practically A.D.C.). I made a suggestion to Uncle Fred about transferring, and he went to an awful lot of trouble to get things fixed up, although when I first asked him I had no idea of any promotion.' With a boyish enthusiasm, he added: 'It will probably mean dispatch-riding, and that will be ripping.'[13]

On Good Friday all the infantrymen began to move out of the camp, leaving the 3rd Light Horse Brigade and the 4th Light Horse Regiment as the sole occupants. It was widely rumoured that the Australians were heading off to meet the enemy. This was real war at last.

On 25 April 1915 the Australian and New Zealand Army Corps (ANZAC) made an amphibious landing on the Gallipoli peninsula, Turkey, and went into action. It did not take long for the news to reach the light horsemen at Mena. The infantrymen that they had seen and mixed with over the recent weeks were now fighting and dying in battle against the Turks. A few days later the brigade shifted closer to Cairo, settling in at the Heliopolis racecourse.

Walter McConnan wrote to his sister:

Our chaps have landed at the Dardanelles now and no doubt will be fighting their way towards Constantinople. We are hoping that light horse will soon be wanted in the operations and no doubt they will. It is rumoured we may be in action before a month. I am not optimistic but hope for the best.[14]

In the few months that the brigade was in Egypt, relations between the brigadier and the brigade major and the three commanding officers had deteriorated. The main cause of trouble was what the regimental officers believed was unnecessary interference in the running of their units. Miell and Brazier became most disgruntled by their treatment. Even White, who maintained better relations with Hughes and Antill, expressed his annoyance: 'At present I am very unpopular with the old chap, the Bullant, and Tintacks. I strongly resented some interference … they must learn we are not infants.'[15]

The 8th's regimental medical officer, Captain Syd Campbell, shared the frustration. The 27-year-old doctor was keen, highly educated and idealistic and had left a promising career in Melbourne to join up. Having attended some of the wounded beginning to arrive from Gallipoli, and seeing the effects of the fighting there, he fumed after Antill ordered an old-style cavalry exercise, 'Brigade drill by trumpet call', for the entire brigade. The huge exercise turned to total chaos. Neither the trumpeters, officers nor any of the troops knew what to do, despite Antill's furious bullying. Afterwards Campbell wrote:

Our officers seem to be getting heartily tired of the course of events in our Brigade and Regiment. Too much Brigade Hqtrs interference with the Regimental training, too much Reg. Hqrtrs interference with squadron OCs. Oh! For some competent officers in the higher commands. What a disappointment a great deal of military life has been to me – the boasted military organisation, keenness, and intelligence.[16]

The troops were becoming anxious to join their countrymen at the fighting front. Colonel White complained: 'They do not want us in Turkey, no place for the light horse, in the meantime we get burned up by the sun, cussed by the Old Man, and eaten by flies. Our tempers are being destroyed.' Miell, White and Brazier got together on the first Sunday in May to discuss their grievances. White noted that 'the three of us were together for the first time really. They also have their little growls and worries, my advice to them was to take their gruel, it is all in the job.'[17]

One of the minor complaints was a carry-over from the Broadmeadows days. There Antill had introduced 'surprise turns out'. On the alarm being given at any time of day or night, the regiments had to muster immediately for his inspection.[18] In Egypt, he and Hughes did a similar thing, usually riding into the regiments' lines about 6 am. Most of the officers and men felt that this was unnecessary and that time could be better spent in more practical training.

A lot of real trouble centred around Brazier. Problems and tensions will always develop whenever a number of people are placed together. But the trouble between Brazier, Antill and Hughes, which came to a head at Heliopolis, went quite a bit further. Brazier had fallen out with Antill while on the troopship and his relationships with him, and with Hughes, only worsened in Egypt. Where other officers may have been prepared to accept advice such as White had given, Brazier would always make his resentments known and would continue to argue the point. In one incident he was publicly upbraided by Hughes for having his second-in-command, Major Alan Love, drill the regiment instead of doing it himself. According to Brazier, Hughes spoke to Love, then sent him away 'like a whipped boy'.[19]

The matter itself many not have been important, but it revealed the far deeper problems between the men. Brazier was sent for in the evening and asked whether he could train the regiment without Love. He was furious and asked to have the whole matter referred to General Sir John Maxwell, the commander in Egypt. His persistence eventually caused the incident to become an embarrassment for Hughes. Brazier now called his relationship with the brigadier and the other staff officers his 'other war', observing: 'I would be better employed fighting Germans than my fellow officers and Head Quarters.'[20] For their part, Hughes and Antill had clearly come to regard Brazier as a troublesome officer and a cause of much frustration.

By now, there was a continuing stream of wounded from Gallipoli. McConnan watched the train-loads of invalids unloading at Heliopolis. 'You see fellows about everywhere with slight wounds. Some of these fellows have only what they stand in available and bloodstains are sometimes visible. I am quite convinced that the story of the Dardanelles will live.'[21]

The sight of the wounded was a reminder of the seriousness of the business they were engaged upon. White addressed his thoughts to his wife: "We hear all sorts of yarns, but the wounded are coming every day. Poor chaps, they have had a bad time.' Knowing that she would be worrying, he made a promise that he would be unable to keep: 'Don't worry or be sad, I am coming back to you and Bill some day, sooner or later, and then we shall be all together again. I must do my work first, and having done that I must do it well. I am coming home for good – no more soldiering – no more going away.'[22]

It was thought that the light horse could be used on Gallipoli as soon as mounted operations became possible. However, the Turks had managed to hold the invaders' advance. At Anzac – the name given to the coastal strip where the Australians and New Zealanders had landed – the enemy had only yielded a narrow toehold on the peninsula. It was decided that all available troops would be necessary if the initiative was to be regained. There were thousands of mounted men (three brigades, plus the 4th Light Horse Regiment from Australia and one brigade and the Otago Mounted Rifles from New Zealand) in Egypt, so it was proposed that they be sent as reinforcements for the infantry battalions. Sir John Maxwell was opposed to the regiments' being broken up, but agreed to their being used dismounted so long as they stayed complete units. The regiments of the 3rd Light Horse Brigade were paraded and asked if they were willing to go to Anzac as dismounted troops. The whole brigade volunteered.

The commanders on Gallipoli now had to consider how they might use these brigades. Light horse regiments were not as large as infantry battalions and they would be further reduced by the need to leave men behind to care for the horses. Still, Maxwell and the light horsemen had their way, and the three brigades all went to Gallipoli intact, with their machine-gunners, signallers and ambulance. The first to go was the 1st Light Horse Brigade, accompanied by the machine-gunners from all brigades. Hughes called a parade of his machine-gun sections and addressed them before they left. Three cheers were given for the departing men.

On 11 May Hughes' brigade was ordered to prepare to move out for the front and those men who would have to stay behind with the horses were nominated. He had no trouble deciding who to leave behind in command of these camp details and the reinforcements – it would be Brazier. No doubt he felt that he would be well rid of this troublesome officer for a while. He placed the departing 10th Regiment under Major Love.

The regiments' saddles and bridles were packed for storage, while spurs and leather leggings were replaced by the 'despised puttees' – woollen strips wound around the lower leg, which invariably defied the novice wearer's attempts to apply them correctly. Even their plumed hats were replaced by high-domed khaki sun helmets. By 14 May the brigade was ready to set off.

Corporal Henry Foss of the 10th Light Horse, who was later killed serving as an infantryman in France, left a record of the move from Heliopolis:

> After stacking all our saddlery … we marched out to the parade ground with our packs up. There we piled our packs, rifles etc … and we were free to wander round for an hour or two. Immediately after tea we again fell in, and after being addressed by Major Love, and giving three cheers for old 'Go Alone', who was staying as Camp Commandant, we marched out in rear of the other regiments; cheering, laughing, singing and joking, we made our way to the railway station, cracking jokes as we passed the Skating Rink Hospital with the wounded who lined the street and windows. The carriages proved to be the old third class cattle truck variety. Within an hour or so all impedimenta were aboard and the train moved out to Alexandria.[23]

The light horsemen were filled with excitement at the prospect of going to the front at last. Brazier watched with a heavy heart as his regiment set off. Later, looking about at the dull job that he was left with, he could only declare: 'Oh Lord. How rotten are things in general.'[24] He felt that he had suffered another cruel injustice.

CHAPTER 7

Gallipoli and Trench Warfare

Two large ships carried the 2nd and 3rd Light Horse Brigades from Alexandria to Gallipoli. The *Menominee* left with the 8th and 9th Regiments, brigade headquarters, the signallers and ambulance, and some New Zealanders. The 10th went on the *Lutzow*, along with the 2nd Light Horse Brigade. The voyage was only to be a short one so the men were packed tight. Reynell, on the *Menominee*, noted: 'There is every comfort for the majority of officers on this transport as she is a passenger boat but the men are terribly crowded.'[1] The *Lutzow* had been regularly ferrying troops and was in a filthy condition.

No sooner were they at sea than there was a submarine scare. Already the Royal Navy had demonstrated the effectiveness of submarines in these waters, and the enemy would do the same. The men stood at watch throughout the voyage. On the evening of 18 May they crowded the rails to see two distant British warships firing their heavy guns against an invisible shore. Soon Cape Helles, the tip of the Gallipoli Peninsula, where the British army had landed, appeared on the horizon. The *Lutzow* was first to arrive off the cape and dropped anchor about a kilometre from shore, giving the troops their first view of the battlefields. The *Menominee* arrived during the day but, while the troops waited, expecting the ships to carry them towards Anzac, they were ordered to Lemnos harbour. It had been decided that the threat of submarines was too great to expose so many troops to this peril.

Ashore, a momentous battle was taking place. The Turks launched large-scale frontal attacks preceded by heavy artillery shelling on the allies' positions. Throughout 19 May the Turkish infantry threw themselves at various parts of the lines but machine-gun and rifle fire shot their attacks to pieces. At Anzac, by the end of the day, over 3,000 of the enemy were believed to have been killed, while the Australians had 628 killed and wounded. The battlefields were strewn with Turkish dead. So intense and persistent were the Turkish assaults that many Australians admitted to an admiration for such determined bravery. It was about this time that the Anzacs began to speak of the enemy in terms of respect as fighting men. In the following days there was a general lull in the action and the light horsemen arrived; they were able to come ashore and get settled in during this relatively quiet period.

The *Lutzow* proceeded to Anzac without the company of the *Menominee*. The ship sailed quietly through the dark night with all lights out. Each man on board knew that on shore men had been fighting and dying, and they peered at the dark mist-covered cliffs with a mixture of curiosity and excitement. All through the night they could hear the rattle of rifle and machine-gun fire coming across the water. They could see the narrow beach and the rugged, eroded, scrub-covered hills and, as daylight broke, the sun glinted on stacks of ammunition boxes and stores, and shadows defined terraces with their rows of dug-outs and the ragged trench lines.

During the afternoon of the 20th, the 2nd Light Horse Brigade, mostly men from New South Wales and Queensland, was disembarked. The 10th Light Horse had to wait until the following day, when the rest of the brigade came up from Lemnos, where it had been put onto speedy destroyers. The troops were then transferred onto barges and pinnaces to make the last short leg of their journey to the shore.

Corporal Henry Foss was found to have a poisoned hand and the doctor would not allow him to land until a few days later. He watched his comrades go while the wounded men were brought on board to take their places. He recorded that, 'they went ashore cheering and laughing, while the wounded chaps alongside me dismally remarked "They'll soon drop that sort of thing".'[2]

The light horsemen landed wearing their smart service dress uniforms and sun helmets, and carrying their packs and rifles, ready to join their countrymen in the great adventure. They received a sober welcome. The place was more like a mining camp, and its occupants, now veterans of a campaign less than a month old, were already weary, tattered and battle-wise. The brigade was guided to its bivouacs without fuss and at dawn next morning stood to arms.

The first mounted units to arrive at Anzac had been Colonel Harry

Chauvel's 1st Light Horse Brigade and the New Zealanders under Colonel Andrew Russell. These brigades had been longer in training and were commanded by senior experienced officers, so they were sent directly into the trenches at Monash Valley and Walker's Ridge as part of the New Zealand and Australian Division under Major General Alexander Godley. More caution was applied to the placement of the two newly arrived brigades. The 2nd Light Horse Brigade was allotted to the 1st Australian Division and was split up through the infantry battalions to gain some experience. Thought had to be given as to how the 3rd Brigade would be employed.

There were some doubts about Hughes' readiness for front-line command, but it was acknowledged that he did have Antill, an experienced regular with war experience, to support him. So the 3rd Light Horse Brigade was initially sent into the northern sector and placed in sections of the line under Chauvel and Russell. This arrangement was soon changed to allow Colonel Russell to be released, and Hughes and his brigade took over on Russell's Top.

The brigade became part of General Godley's division. The general was a tall slender man with an aristocratic air. In many respects he represented the 'haw haw' type of British senior officer so often lampooned by the Australians. He was of Anglo-Irish descent, from a military family of no great wealth, and had a close and important association with the New Zealanders. Shortly before the war he had gone to New Zealand to organise and command the forces there, and he was already known to some of the senior Australian officers. His was one of the two divisions at the original landing on 25 April, making up the corps (a corps is usually two or more divisions) from which the name Anzac was derived.

The 9th Light Horse was sent directly up to Walker's Ridge and on to Russell's Top, where the New Zealanders had earlier established themselves. They were to relieve the Auckland Mounted Rifles. Reynell went on ahead and, in a letter sent home, described what he found:

When I was looking round one trench that we were to relieve I suddenly came on a dead New Zealander in an advanced state of decomposition that had been dragged into the trench by the NZ men with a crooked stick. It was a very unpleasant object and I was glad they had buried him by the time our men came to occupy the trench.[3]

White also had a look around: 'I went through the trenches, it's impossible to describe them, they are wonderful. In some places they are only 20 yards from the Turks. The Turks are very good at snipe shooting. There are lots of dead Turks about, and the smell is awful, also lots of our chaps, it's impossible to get them in.'[4]

The 10th Light Horse moved in below Walker's Ridge and reported for orders to the 1st Light Horse Brigade, while the 8th Regiment went up to the ridge two days later to relieve the Wellington Mounted Rifles.

Tom Kidd was 45 years old when he left his wife and family, and a settled position as a Geraldton accountant, to join the AIF. He had been quick to rush to the bugle's call, just as he had 15 years earlier when he went off to the South African War. He was now an officer in the 10th Light Horse.

We removed camp on the morning of May 23 to Shrapnel Valley. We do not have transport facilities on Gallipoli as all ranks carry everything on their backs. Officers dress similar to the troopers carrying ruck-sacks (or packs) and wearing similar equipment, but without rifles. By means of a big communications sap we pass across hills behind GOC headquarters until we reach a long valley which commences at the steep hills [and] runs right down to the sea opening out on to the beach.[5]

The one thing that immediately struck the men, especially as they came closer to the front line and the adjoining no-man's-land, was a pervasive stench. The dead, particularly the Turks killed in their attack of 19 May, lay thick in front of the trenches. Lieutenant Kidd continued: 'The atmosphere was heavily charged with the smell of rotting humans which was until one became accustomed to it, inclined to render you a bit bilious.'[6] Not only was it unpleasant, it was also posing a very serious health problem.

Fortunately, a remarkable thing happened on the 24th: the fighting stopped to allow the dead to be buried. The two sides had managed to arrange a nine-hour armistice. 'It's quite strange not to hear shooting,' noted Colonel White.[7]

During this break in the fighting, William Cameron, of the 9th Light Horse, decided that he would hop out to have a look around:

Have done so and the sight is gruesome and peculiar. Its awfulness is appalling. Thousands of bodies lie rotting in the intervening space between the enemy's and our trenches about 200 yards, and the stench is sickening. The burial party have a horrible job, yet the whole thing is peculiar in that Turk, Britain [*sic*], or Australian are intermingled in a common task of placing out of sight the bodies of dead comrades, and in a few short hours this will cease and each will be in his own trench, each doing his best to add to the already large list.[8]

The 10th Light Horse provided burial parties to dispose of the dead from both sides in front of Quinn's Post, which was already a notorious killing ground. Next day Reynell noted that in his area 'all the dead were buried – the ground on which they were lying rotting still stinks badly but it is better and will no doubt be all right in a day or two'.[9]

Following the repulse of the Turkish attack of 19 May, the British commanders at Anzac began to feel that their defences were strong enough to resist any Turkish effort to try to push them back into the sea. The Turks too now believed that they could hold the British and empire troops in the small area at Anzac. Neither side was willing to acknowledge that a stalemate was all that was now possible, and Birdwood was already considering the likely success of a new offensive. Any British optimism was dulled on 25 May, when HMS *Triumph* was sunk by an enemy submarine. The battleship had stood off Anzac, in view of the troops ashore, providing a symbol of British naval might. The light horsemen on Walker's Ridge watched as boats rushed to rescue crewmen, then saw the big ship slip below the surface.

For several days the 10th Light Horse provided parties on rotation at Pope's Hill and Quinn's Post, two of the most dangerous spots at Anzac. Both places were critical for the security of the entire Anzac area and at each the Australian and Turkish trenches almost ran into each other.

Lieutenant Kidd had watched the enemy attack at Quinn's Post only a day or so before he went up there:

The enemy lost heavily and I myself saw a huge heap of mangled and dismembered Turks dragged out of our own trenches. They lay in heaps in view of all of us for days before they could be removed and presented a sickening sight. However we became used to it. It was good schooling for the game of war.[10]

The brigade's first fight was a limited affair and came on 30 May, when parties from the 10th Light Horse made an assault on two positions at Quinn's Post. It had been observed that the enemy had occupied and were fortifying two craters immediately in front of the Australians' trenches. Fifty men were ordered to make the attack. Everyone knew the danger, but when told that two officers would be needed, Kidd responded: 'Put me down for one and Colpitts for the other.' Kidd later confided that 'at this time the attack appeared like a forlorn hope … [I] handed Doc Bentley my paybook with money, binoculars, and last but not least a letter to my wife before we lined up.'[11]

At five minutes past one o'clock the officers led their men in scrambling charges into the Turks' new positions. They took them after wild fighting and then, for three hours, held on against counter-attacks. The Turks threw 30 bombs into Kidd's trench; these were grabbed and returned. Almost every man was wounded in the fierce melee. One Turk managed to fire at Kidd from about 5 metres. The round grazed his nose and cheek, leaving him momentarily blinded by blood and dirt. Eventually, realising his position was hopeless he led his men in a desperate dash back to their own lines. Colpitts was able to hold out long enough to be reinforced and for a tunnel to be dug to tie-in the captured crater with Quinn's Post.

It was a brief but heroic effort. Of the 46 men who took part, only 14 came out unscathed. Lieutenant Colpitts was evacuated wounded, but Kidd managed to stay on duty. The next day he noted: 'Find my limbs full of bomb splinters. Joe Scott picks them out with a knife. My left eye blackens, partially closed. Left side of face all bruised.' At first the strain did not show, but the reaction came shortly afterwards when he went down to the beach for a rest: 'Go for a swim. Collapse on platform just as good old Doc Bentley predicted would happen.'[12]

This attack at Quinn's Post was one of the few offensive actions undertaken by members of the brigade during its first ten weeks at Anzac. Shortly after this the 10th Light Horse moved up to Russell's Top so that the brigade's three regiments were now all together for the first time since Egypt.

Russell's Top came off the main Sari Bair range and could be reached up a long and very steep route from the beach area along Walker's Ridge. It was exhausting work to carry any load along the narrow track, which in places ran close to sheer cliff edges. Monash Valley pinched into Russell's Top at the narrowest point confronting the Turkish positions, on one side

of what was called 'The Nek'. Evidently some South African War veteran
had named the place in the early days of the fighting. A *nek* was a local
name for a feature on military maps during that war. The regiments took
their turns in the forward trenches and the support lines, where they were
employed improving and extending the defences. The men soon began
to fall into the routine of trench warfare: working, manning trenches and
resting. Jack Dean's lifelong recollections of this period were of 'digging,
tunnelling, getting out dirt, and putting in mines'. He remembered the dust
and grime, poor food, and the flies. The continual digging often exposed the
buried dead.[13]After several weeks of these foul conditions, he succumbed
to enteric fever and became one of the 8th Light Horse's long list of men
evacuated through illness. In addition to the squalid unhealthy conditions,
the enemy was always there to shell, bomb or threaten attack.

The regiments usually worked on the basis of a fortnight in the trenches,
followed by a similar period of rest. Rest simply meant a move closer to the
beach. It was sometimes better to be in the trenches than down on the shore.
Foss records that 'the trenches during our stay were particularly safe, and
though continually ordered to keep our heads down etc, these orders only
excited our amusement. Fact was that Abdul found it too risky to fire at us,
but turned his attention mainly to the beach.'[14]

Despite this snipers were always a danger, and there was a steady stream
of wounded sent down from the trenches to the hospital tents. Shelling was
a greater problem though, and while a well-directed salvo often caused
no casualties, a stray shell might come over at any time and create death
and havoc. The light horsemen discovered that there was one Turkish
75-millimetre gun, claimed to be of French manufacture, which clearly had
Russell's Top as one of its dedicated targets.

The selection of weapons available to the trench soldier at this time
was limited. The Lewis gun and Stokes mortar had not yet made their
appearance, nor had poison gas or flame-throwers been introduced here.
The main arms were the Maxim machine-gun, the rifle and bayonet, and
hand grenades. The Australians had virtually no experience with grenades –
'bombs', as they were called then – until they arrived at Anzac, and then the
supply was always short. The very effective Mills bomb, which remained
in use until the Korean War, did not appear until late in the campaign. A
number of more primitive types, cast in foundries in Egypt and Malta, were
used, and these were supplemented by crude 'jam-tin' bombs made from
scraps in a workshop on the beach. The Turks always seemed better off.

The Australians had the impression, although they were wrong, that the enemy had large stocks of bombs. They did have iron spherical grenades and were skilled in using them; most of these relied largely on their blast and were more likely to maim than to kill outright. They also had an effect on morale. McConnan recalled some enemy bombs exploding harmlessly high above him: 'it is curious that each bomb gave me a kind of shock which took a minute or two to pass.'[15]

Bombs were in constant use in the front line, and opposing trenches were sometimes within throwing range. The Turkish bombs often had long fuses which, if one was quick and game enough, enabled them to be thrown back. Many brave men were mutilated or killed attempting this. One of the types issued to the light horsemen was an old model with a brass body, around which was an iron fragmentation band. It was thrown using its cane or wooden handle and detonated on impact. It was dangerous to throw from the confines of a trench, and awkward to carry. Another type, made of cast iron, was similar to the Turks' 'cricket ball' bombs and was ignited by a five-second fuse.

Digging was an unrelenting and exhausting business. New trenches, saps and tunnels were dug, while existing ones had to be deepened or widened. Colonel White commented that it was a far cry from the type of work that light horsemen had joined up to do: 'It is such rotten soldiering. Trench warfare is the limit, so different to what we expected.' Earlier he had marvelled at the extent of the trenches: 'They are a maze, a network, and quite easy to get lost in.'[16]

Eating, sleeping and swimming – these were the few simple pleasures available to the soldiers. Although water was always short, the food was adequate but rarely interesting. Tinned meat, called 'bully beef', and biscuits were the staple. This was usually supplemented with vegetables and occasionally bread and fresh meat. Cooks did not usually accompany the squadrons into the trenches, where cooking was often done in small groups. Rissoles made from bully beef, ground-up biscuits, some 'Indian meal' and locally gathered thyme were popular. Rum was issued, but its arrival was not very regular. In late May William Cameron of the 9th Light Horse happily recorded: 'Enjoyed a very good breakfast of fried "Bully", carrots, parsnips, and onions, with army biscuits and jam; cocoa to drink.'[17] On another occasion he wrote: 'Whilst our men were cooking their break-fast this morning two shells lobbed right on the parapet flattening out two men and covering one right over; the breakfast suffered considerably, but we had to have it or nothing. We were eating sand and gravel with our curry stew.'

On 6 June the 9th Light Horse was able to hold a church parade. A week later a similar parade, held by the 8th Regiment, was disrupted by shell fire. Cameron was a keen soldier and a devout Christian. On a previous Sunday he had observed the Sabbath as best he could:

Here I am ... having had a shave, a wash and mouth cleaning, all in one cup of water, and general change, and feel quite Sunday-like, while outside and all around is the thunder of guns, the whistle and scream of bullets and shells. Have been spending this couple of hours reading passages from my Bible, and a feeling of calm and confidence comes over me.

After the first church parade he wrote:

I have never seen these men listen as they have done this day; notwithstanding their outward apparent callousness, these rough-hewn men have an undercurrent of thought which is only brought to the top on occasions such as this, when, more than anywhere else, they are brought to face with the stern fact that, we know not what a day or an hour may bring forth. Truly God has greatly blessed us, and we are truly grateful.

The possibility of sudden death, or mutilation, was always present on Anzac, as the evidence all around showed. One of the most horrible memories from that time was the exposing of decaying corpses while extending the trenches, and it happened often. Trooper Jack Dean recalled the unpleasantness of it 70 years afterwards, and there are numerous contemporary accounts. Colonel White reported: 'We are always finding dead men, it's all very awful: The smell of the dead is not nice.' Major Thomas Redford, one of his officers, wrote: 'While sapping and trenching we continually come across dead men.'[18] Another in the regiment, Tom Austin, wrote:

It was quite a common sight to pass through portions of the saps, and see a pair of boots, the feet of a dead man, or his hands or else some boards passing through the sides and holding the bodies in place. In no time we grew callous to such items and the boards often contained epitaphs inscribed there by some 'hard cases'.[19]

Alexander White was a popular and inspiring officer, but in the privacy of his dug-out he revealed his horror in his diary: 'Dear little wife and kiddie I seem so far away from you all; I do not want to speak about the war; it's horrible. If I let myself think too much about it my nerves would go. Have seen things and done things I want to forget.'[20]

June arrived and the weather was becoming warmer. With the heat came masses of flies and the spread of sickness and disease. By July a health crisis was developing. Sanitation became an increasingly vital concern, and the medical officers had to work hard to see that every effort was made to improve the conditions. Dysentery and diarrhoea spread through the regiments, which were quickly weakened by the high sickness rate and the consequent evacuations of sick to the hospitals.

Tom Austin recorded that 'the flies and vermin were becoming intolerable and the Medical Officer was at his wits end to know how to cope with disease owing to the very limited facilities at his disposal'.[21] In the first days of July the 8th Light Horse moved down to its rest camp. 'The men at this time were suffering very badly from a vomiting sickness with septic sores.' The latter, said Austin, 'is a kind of scurvy and is similar to an Australian scourge known as "Barcoo Rot", known to every bushman West of the Darling.'[22] A few days later he joined the sick parade and was among those who had to be taken off Anzac.

The dwindling strength of the regiments through death, sickness and wounds was now a major concern. Reinforcements arrived but they were not keeping pace with the losses. The older men usually suffered most, and Hughes and Miell were soon ill. The 10th Light Horse could not maintain sufficient officers as evacuations rose. By 22 June, 237 men were away from the brigade. When the 9th Regiment went back into the trenches in mid-July, every man was placed in the front line as there were not enough to provide the usual supports. Even men who were managing to hang on were becoming noticeably weaker.

A few weeks later Lieutenant Charles Carthew reflected on the state of the 8th Light Horse: 'Our old Regt. That fine body of men that marched through town a short time ago would make a very poor show now – that is if we had only those that are left of the original crowd. Don't think I have ten men of my old original crowd and not one Non Com[missioned officer]. I'd give something to have them here today.'[23]

As the days dragged into weeks, and June slipped into July, a psychological change came over the soldiers clinging to the hot, dusty and dangerous cliffs on this narrow and short stretch of the Turkish peninsula. Many weeks earlier these men had grumbled about long rides in the desert, at having to dig trenches and then fill them in, had resented the brigade major's early morning inspections, and had complained about the boredom of the training camps. These worries seemed to be of small consequence now. They had wanted to see action, even if it meant being separated from their horses. Now they had it. They had sought adventure, and possibly glory, but found themselves dirty, thirsty, constantly digging and tunnelling, living in scooped-out burrows, having to stand-to before each dawn, and their field of activities limited to the slopes of this rugged shoreline. Of even greater concern was the alarming spread of disease and illness and the constant threat of death or possibly maiming from the ever-present enemy. Evidence of their mortality was all around them. They lived among the graves, looked out over rotting corpses, and had their senses assailed by the constant stench.

Overriding all the soldiers' worries was the realisation that there was no end in sight. Most of these men had been prepared to be away from home maybe a year or so, to perhaps face a major battle, and even risk death. Now it appeared that they would stay on Anzac, fearing an attack that could come at any time, and with no conclusion possible for them beyond serious illness, injury or death.

CHAPTER 8

Walker's Ridge and Russell's Top

The harsh conditions, and spread of disease, affected even the fittest young men at Anzac. Fred Hughes, now 57 years old, found them debilitating and could offer little resistance to the prevailing illnesses. Soon his health broke down. He lasted at his post for the first few weeks, but in June had to be evacuated suffering from pneumonia. He was in Egypt for a short time then spent most of the month on a hospital ship. No sooner had he returned than he was ill again and had to be sent back to the ship for a further week during July.

Hughes' declining health and lack of fitness prevented him from taking a full and active role in the command of his brigade. Largely owing to this, and an awareness of the trouble he was having with a couple of his officers, most notably Brazier, he lost the trust of his superiors. Charles Bean, in a discreet footnote in the official history, says Birdwood now had little confidence in Hughes.[1] When pressed in 1928 by Wilfrid Kent Hughes to justify this statement, Bean responded bluntly: 'All I can say is … the authority for this is absolute.'[2] Clearly Bean had been told this by Birdwood, or one of his most senior staff.

With the ageing Hughes unable to give proper attention to his work, most of the responsibility fell to Antill, who, it was acknowledged, became the main influence in the command of the brigade. Probably because the brigade major had a reputation for being strict and experienced, it was felt that there was no need to replace the brigadier. Senior officers who met Antill on Gallipoli were initially impressed by him as he conformed more to the style of the professional British army officers than most of the other Australians whom they encountered.

Reports of Antill's work at Anzac spoke of his efficiency. He kept the headquarters staff working smoothly, there were few discipline problems, and the brigade's trenches were among the best to be seen. While he certainly had ambitions to obtain the command of the brigade for himself, Antill did nothing to undermine Hughes' position. Writing to his brother, he described Hughes as 'a fine gentleman and my strongest and best friend – straight as a line'.[3] In return, Hughes seems to have had full faith in him.

Birdwood should have taken steps to have Hughes retired. But it was an era in which it was not unusual for a senior officer to be retained despite the evidence showing that he was unsuitable. Declining ability and fading reputations were often overlooked. In a system where background and influence still held much weight, the simplest course was to take no action. Bean criticised the failure to remove these officers, but observed that it was a very common practice to do nothing in such circumstances.[4] The practice of propping up ineffective commanders had become so ingrained in the British military system that it spilled over into the colonial and dominion forces, and was acknowledged as a matter of fact by Colonel Hubert Foster, the Director of Military Science at Sydney University before the war, in writing on the 'Principles of command'. He wrote: 'Only one man can command. It is true that the nominal Commander has not always been this one man, owing to some physical, intellectual or moral deficiency in his character.' He added, 'however, it is essential that the Chief must rely on one man only'.[5] On Anzac Hughes had to some extent become, in Foster's words, the brigade's 'nominal commander'.

Another commander too old to manage in the conditions on Gallipoli was Major James O'Brien, the 8th Light Horse's second-in-command, who was also in his fifties. He was continually ill and had to be replaced. Miell, the commanding officer of the 9th Light Horse, also had health problems and had to go away for a short time. On another occasion he was wounded while asleep in his dug-out. It was not serious and he was back on duty after a week.

Carew Reynell, the second in command, continued to play an important role in the management of the 9th Light Horse. He was an exceptional soldier and had quickly gained a reputation as being quite fearless. He claimed as a great uncle a distinguished British officer at the battle of Waterloo, and he had a love of military history. His wife later wrote: 'My husband had always been an ardent soldier. When he was 12 years of age he had read every book he could get about Military History including Napier's

Peninsula War – which he knew very thoroughly.'[6] Reynell's father had prevented him going off to the South African War because he was then still in his teens. He became an active militia officer and was a major in the 22nd Light Horse Regiment when the war commenced. He liked all aspects of soldiering – one of his sergeants complained that he had a 'partiality for drill', even on Gallipoli, and was inspired by what he saw as his role in the great military events taking place around him.

If courage was part of the Reynell family's heritage, it was most evident in the generations which served in the world wars. Carew Reynell was to be killed on Gallipoli in an action in which he abandoned all caution. His son, Richard, who was then just two years old, served as a pilot in the Royal Air Force and died on 7 September 1940 while fighting in the Battle of Britain. May Reynell, herself a tireless war worker, lost her husband, brother and son in the wars. When writing of the circumstances of his death, Hughes had to say that Reynell 'was too keen – if such is possible'.[7]

The last week in June was a tough one for the brigade and saw the 8th and 9th Regiments involved in their first big fight, with Reynell playing a notable part. But in the lead-up to this some casualties were suffered.

On the 27th, the enemy's artillery commenced firing on Walker's Ridge, and for a while the shells fell heavily upon the 8th Light Horse in the trenches opposite The Nek. Within half an hour seven men were killed and 15 wounded. The regimental headquarters was badly hit and Lieutenant Colonel White was wounded in the head; his second-in-command, Major Ernest Gregory, who was trying to organise stretcher parties, and the adjutant, Captain Joseph Crowl, were both killed.

The enemy gunners could hardly have hoped for a better bag. The loss of these prominent officers, who were central to the operation of the regiment, was a severe shock. Gregory's experience had been admired – he had served 15 years, had recently spent six months with the British cavalry in India, and afterwards was in command of a militia light horse regiment – and Crowl's ability respected. Because no regular soldiers of appropriate rank had been immediately available for the post of adjutant when the 8th Light Horse was being formed, 'Terry' Crowl, a second lieutenant from the militia, had been temporarily appointed. He performed so well, and had shown such promise, that he had been confirmed in the position and promoted.

Many in the regiment were affected by the officers' deaths, including Trooper Alexander Borthwick. 'I will be glad to take my uniform off, never to wear it again. To see a strong vigorous man like Captain Crowle [*sic*] have the life crushed out of him in a second by a shell is enough to make war revolting to any man.'[8] A large group gathered around the graves of both men when they were buried side by side down near the beach.

Major Arthur Deeble was promoted into Gregory's position and, for the moment, also filled in for Colonel White. Regarded as more fastidious than efficient, he was a university-educated suburban school principal who had enthusiastically devoted much of his spare time to soldiering. On Gallipoli he would have to face the raw edge of battle until, finally, he was taken off ill in September.[9]

White was evacuated with his wound, and later wrote: 'This awful day. They shelled us with the French "75" at 5 am. I was hit at 5.30. Crowl and Gregory within a few minutes of each other – poor chaps they never knew what hit them. It was Gregory's birthday too.'[10] With some relief, he added: 'They put me on a Hospital ship where the piece of shell was taken out, a hot bath, pyjamas, and sleep.' At least he was free from the wild fighting which soon followed.

The shelling was resumed at intervals as a preliminary to a massed Turkish assault across The Nek in the early morning of 30 June. On a black, stormy night the enemy commenced with a feint against Quinn's Post. Meanwhile artillery rounds fell on Russell's Top, which was then subjected to heavy machine-gun and rifle fire. At midnight the men in the forward saps reported movement on the enemy's front and those in the firing line and support trenches were alerted. Men began to file into position and stood shoulder to shoulder on the fire-steps, while behind them machine-gunners peered forward looking for signs of movement. About 15 minutes passed, then the Turks appeared, rising from the trenches and rushing forward in a massed attack.

The Australians were ready and met the enemy, as they came across The Nek, with a withering fire. Maxim guns, firing on fixed lines with well-measured ranges, scythed down dozens of them. Still they came on, many stumbling unaware into the forward saps, where sharp actions were fought with bombs and bayonets. For a while B Squadron of the 8th Light Horse took the brunt, but it never faltered, its concentrated fire dropping the enemy in front of them. The firing line was packed with riflemen, while many of the support troops, unable to find a place, climbed out of the back of the trenches to get a better shot. The Australians fired and reloaded, recharging their magazines like machines. Captain Archibald McLaurin, one of the few senior officers left in the 8th Light Horse, led a counter-attack to recover one of the main saps, which had been overrun.

On the left the enemy got into the long shallow front sap, which had been only lightly held, and about 50 of them crossed, continuing deep into the Australians' positions. Reynell, revolver in hand, then quickly gathered a party and rushed up a communications trench, fighting his way into the front sap. Shots were exchanged at about three metres. More men followed, shooting and bombing, until the line was regained.

In the 9th Light Horse, Sergeant Cameron was leading his troop forward when he was ordered to reinforce the machine-gun post at Turk's Point, which was threatened by the enemy, who had broken through. 'The firing at this point was very heavy, and I lost one man before we got into position. Then we extended along the ridge and in doing so lost two more. It fairly rained hail [of bullets] there and they even succeeded in getting between our main trench and posts, but these were soon accounted for.'[11]

About this time the enemy tried to outflank the 8th Light Horse by moving around below the ridge on the right. They were seen and dealt with by bombs and by machine-guns from across on Pope's Hill. By 2 am, the Turkish attack had been destroyed. Despite this, another assault was launched later in the morning. It was shot down as soon as the men had left the trenches. The Australians' discipline never wavered, and the enemy, by attacking on such a narrow front, had no chance against both machine-guns and rapid, concentrated rifle fire. Captain 'Naish' Callary, of the 9th Light Horse wrote:

> The Turks had a bad time. Our fellows said it reminded them of shooting rabbits running around. They were repulsed with severe losses as the morning showed when one could have a good look. Nothing but dead Turks all over the place. One gets used to the smell. How callous one gets. Such sights one sees and being so common and frequent makes one frightfully hard.[12]

At the height of the fighting the killing became automatic and impersonal. Walter McConnan wrote about it to his father: 'Our rifle-fire not only checked them but piled them up in heaps. Of course a good many got away but our bag was good, I reckoned on a couple for my share. This was the most exciting time we had enjoyed till recently.'[13] Reading this letter

70 years afterwards, his daughter commented: 'at times I find it hard to reconcile some [of] his remarks with the truly gentle person he was'.[14]

Morning was a sobering experience. Sergeant Cameron, who had lost three of his men in the fighting, wrote:

> I went around the trenches in the morning, and the sight that met one's gaze was horrible. Dead Turks and some not quite dead were lying about like rabbits after a night's poison had been laid. We rescued the wounded by throwing out ropes to which they fastened themselves and were drawn in; the dead near the trenches were dragged in and buried.[15]

The light horse casualties had been light: seven men killed and 19 wounded. The enemy's losses amounted to hundreds, and dozens of them were buried by the Australians. The regiments remained alert but in the following days the Turks, obviously stunned by the scale of their defeat, were quiet. Captain George Wieck recalled how 'scarcely a shot was fired at Russell's Top during the whole of 30 June, and the men moved freely where previously it was death to venture'.[16] The light horsemen were kept busy burying the dead, and cleaning up and repairing the trenches. The numerous bodies lying out in no-man's-land could not be reached and remained there until the end of the campaign. Within days the stench from these decaying corpses enveloped Russell's Top.

An interpreter from Godley's headquarters, Aubrey Herbert, best known as a British member of parliament and a renowned Middle East traveller, was sent up to help bring in any Turks who might be still be lying wounded in front of the parapets. Scholarly, adventurous, and quite un-military looking, Herbert was one of the more eccentric members of the staff. Afterwards he often visited Russell's Top and became good friends with Carew Reynell and young Kent Hughes. The entry in his diary about the day's work provides a picture of the death and destruction following battle:

> We found a first-rate Australian, Major Reynell. We went through the trenches, dripping with sweat; it was a boiling hot day. We had to crawl through a secret sap over a number of dead Turks, some of whom were in a ghastly condition, headless and covered with flies.

Then out from the darkness into another sap, with a dead Turk to walk over. The Turkish trenches were 30 yards off, and the dead lay between the two lines. When I called I was answered at once by a Turk. He said he could not move … I gave him a drink, and Reynell and I carried him in, stumbling over the dead among whom he lay.[17]

Another occasional visitor was Charles Bean. Little escaped the notice of this lanky bespectacled man as he moved around the headquarters or through the trench lines. He developed a deep admiration for the types of Australians he found here, although he was never one of them, and was always awkward in the company of ordinary soldiers. Lieutenant Colonel White had been unimpressed by Bean and believed that if Donald McDonald, a Melbourne correspondent who had gone to the South African War, was covering the campaign instead of Bean, 'you would have some splendid accounts of our life here'.[18] White knew that one of Bean's early despatches sent from Egypt, describing the wild behaviour of some of the first contingent, had been resented by the troops. He would never know that the author would one day immortalise the AIF in his remarkable official history.

In their attack across The Nek, the Turks had demonstrated, to their great cost, that it was impossible to cross this narrow stretch of ground in the face of machine-guns and massed rifle fire. In such a narrow space the advantage lay all too heavily with the defenders, regardless of which side of no-man's-land they stood. The reputation of the ground in front of The Nek was now firmly established as a notorious killing field. The Turks had already given the place the name Jessarit Tepe (Hill of Valour).

It was the weaponry available, abetted by the terrain, which in the end set the nature of the campaign, and here the machine-gun dominated. Although both sides had more than one type of machine-gun, the main one each used on Gallipoli was essentially the same, the Maxim gun. The British Vickers gun, an improved version, was also beginning to come available. The Maxim was cumbersome and heavy because of its distinctive water cooling-jacket enclosing the barrel, but it was also reliable and deadly. It could pour out about 500 rounds per minute, and be fired over sights up to 2000–2300 metres. From a fixed mounting it could be set to shoot on predetermined targets on call. Employed in enfilade, a few guns in defence provided an impenetrable zone of fire.

On 2 July the 9th Light Horse was relieved and moved down to Rest Gully. The 8th Regiment followed a couple of days later and, while there, was reunited with its commanding officer who resumed duty with his head still heavily bandaged. When White saw the carnage from the battle, which had taken place in his absence, he said he could only feel sorry for the Turks.

It was little over a fortnight after the 8th Light Horse suffered the loss of two of its senior officers that tragedy struck again with the death of Captain Campbell, the regiment's doctor. He, White and Dale had walked the kilometre to the beach to have an evening swim. It had been a quiet day and this was usually the safest time. However, while the men were undressing on a barge, a Turkish shell struck, tearing off Campbell's lower legs before exploding and wounding others nearby. White and Dale were stunned. Campbell was rushed to a medical tent, but little could be done. He died on a hospital ship early next morning, 14 July.[19] Colonel White, having cheated death once again, wrote home:

> A sad, sad, day, poor dear Campbell, how we all loved him. Doctor, soldier, gentleman, friend ... he was always so gentle, sympathetic and kind. The men loved him; the officers called him a man. Dear straight upright clean living Campbell, cut off just as your splendid life and career was just beginning, why should it be so? You who could so ill be spared to us. God comfort your parents; the whole Regiment mourns for you. Oh war is horrible.[20]

Despite the action and ordeals on Anzac, the brigade's staff was still bothered by the attitude of Brazier back in Egypt, his lack of communication, and other petty problems. Brazier was now insisting that he took his orders from the local base commandant. In particular, a furore developed over the use of four motor cars the brigade had left behind. When Antill heard that Brazier was using one of the vehicles, he wrote demanding that they all be locked away and the keys sent to him on Anzac. Instead, Brazier referred the matter to the local commandant who approved the cars being used.

The situation reached new depths while Hughes was away from Gallipoli and convalescing in Egypt. He visited Brazier and stayed overnight at the camp. Brazier saw that Hughes was feeling the strain of active service and thought he looked 'a wreck'. Next morning the brigadier asked for the four cars to accompany him to Cairo so that he could collect some troops' comforts. Instead, when he reached the Australian Base Office he dismissed the drivers and sent the cars on to the motor transport company. After he left, Brazier, who had been tipped off, simply went back to the base commandant and obtained authority to have the vehicles returned to him. Hughes, of course, was furious when he heard of this further defiance.

Hughes and Antill were also not very happy with Major Alan Love, who was acting in command of the 10th Light Horse. It was thought that he bore many of Brazier's attitudes. He became unpopular, and lost a lot of support within the regiment, when he devised a scheme to send out a party of about ten men to attack, and then destroy with explosives, an enemy strongpoint called Snipers' Nest. Kidd, who had been lucky to survive when he led the attack at Quinn's post, was very critical of the plan which showed little regard for the lives of the men. He reported that the 'party came back quicker than they went. To perform the job in one night under the nose of a strong Turkish outpost appears to me to have emanated from a hysterical brain.'[21] Foss described it as 'an extremely risky and somewhat inglorious episode.'[22]

A week before receiving his movement orders, Brazier got a note from Love:

> I am informed by Brigade HQrs that you are expected here any day and the sooner the better for they are worrying the life out of me. A CO has not only to fight the enemy but the staff as well. I have been bad with diarrhoea for about 14 days and am just about played out. I understand the Brigadier was very annoyed with you over something, hence his decision to relieve you and get you over here.[23]

Against the last sentence Brazier scribbled triumphantly: 'Motor Cars – he got licked.' Love continued:

> Antill is as great a bully as ever and leads us a cat and dog life – I understand there is a possibility of his getting command of the brigade if the Brigadier again breaks down. What ho, then! When you come take my advice and bring fruit, cocoa, coffee, and tin soups or such like, as there is nothing here, but tin dog.

Brazier left Alexandria on 27 July, handing his duties over to Major Daly of the 9th Light Horse, and arrived at Anzac three days later to resume command of his regiment. Hughes apprised him of the situation and escorted him around the trenches on Russell's Top. For the moment their mutual animosity was thinly concealed.

Throughout July the three regiments' casualties through enemy action and sickness continued to mount. On 12 July, McFarlane, the staff captain, was hit. He received a severe leg wound which required his being sent away and eventually returned to Australia. He was replaced by another regular officer, but when he became ill young Kent Hughes was appointed to act in the position. The replacement of a veteran professional soldier by the brigadier's 20-year-old nephew, who had only held his rank of second lieutenant for a few weeks, has to be seen as a weakening of the brigade's command capacity and a strengthening of Antill's hand. One can only speculate on what role McFarlane might have played had he been present during the charge at The Nek, but his experience must have been missed.

One of the 8th Light Horse officers commented that: 'Our acting staff captain Billy Kent Hughes was a mere boy, very good natured and thoroughly inexperienced. Like the Brigadier, he left most things to the brigade major, who largely trusted to luck and countermanded his own orders.'[24]

Kent Hughes was a remarkable young man. He had been awarded a Rhodes scholarship before leaving for the war, was later an Olympic athlete, served in both wars and became a well known member of state and federal parliaments. He was eventually promoted to brigade major of the 3rd Light Horse Brigade and performed well throughout the later desert campaign. Antill described him as 'a fine boy,' adding, 'we took him from the ranks'.[25] In mid-June Kent Hughes received a minor bullet wound to the arm and was sent off to the hospital ship, where he joined his uncle for a couple of days. He was also to see his father, who had obtained a commission in the Australian Army Medical Corps and was now attached to No. 3 Australian General Hospital on Lemnos; they met briefly on the beach during a visit his father made to Anzac.[26]

While more senior officers were watching Hughes' performance, he was assessing that of his own officers. The two eldest commanding officers, Brazier and Miell, had not impressed Hughes to the extent that White had done, and he increasingly felt that Brazier was unfit for his position. From his three regiments he believed that White, Reynell, and Todd of the 10th Light Horse were the best of those he had available.

Major Tom Todd was an important member of his regiment. Although a 41-year-old city accountant, he had shown that he was not out of place among the hardiest of his unit's bushmen. Described as 'over six feet in height, with a powerful, resonant voice and a tremendous virility and energy', he had learnt his soldiering with the New Zealanders as a young lieutenant on the South African veldt.[27] He was one of that war's early colonial heroes, being awarded the Distinguished Service Order for his work during 1900. His experience had been invaluable when the 10th Light Horse was being formed and trained. At home in Perth he had been called 'the life and soul of Claremont' camp.[28] He was quickly promoted and given command of A Squadron. There was an uneasiness in Brazier's relations with Todd, whom he must have seen as a reminder of his own limited experience and lack of active service.

CHAPTER 9

The New Offensive

Like the preceding naval attacks, the land offensive, which had commenced in late April and included the landing at Anzac, had failed to obtain its objective. The distasteful option of withdrawal had been quickly discarded as it was still imagined that if only sufficient force were applied the peninsula might yet be taken. Accordingly, the British command decided that more troops were needed to allow a fresh large-scale attack to be mounted. At the ordinary soldiers' level, it was necessary that a 'holding on' mood not be allowed to develop and that the offensive attitude be maintained.

Birdwood believed that success lay in forcing a breakout from the north at Anzac to capture the dominating heights of Chunuk Bair and Hill 971. The commander-in-chief, General Sir Ian Hamilton, whose optimism too often over-rode reality, was convinced of the value of this approach as a vital part of the larger plan to take the peninsula and open the way for the Royal Navy to reach Constantinople. With the promise of further troops, mostly British, he saw a chance to regain the initiative. The problem was that the Anzac area was cramped and hard to supply, and hardly constituted a firm position from which to make a concentrated breakout.

The Sari Bair heights could be attacked from either of two approaches: up from Anzac along the spine of the range, requiring the capture of The Nek, or directly up the seaward slopes of the high hills. Birdwood's plans called for both these approaches to be used, in particular, a left-hook advance up the valleys and gullies to gain the heights. But a proper base would also be needed for any operations that would follow. And so further landings would also be made a bit further north, along the coast towards Suvla. Landings there would also protect the flank of the attacks on the heights. While the Anzac and Suvla endeavours were linked, each was a distinct operation under separate command. The main breakout efforts from Anzac would also need to be supported by some secondary or diversionary attacks. All of this was set to commence on 6 August, when the moon was in its final quarter.

The men holding the beach and Anzac perimeter became aware that more troops were expected, and a big push likely, when they saw new accommodation terraces being built and water supplies being prepared. By the end of July there was more evidence that something was about to happen. Tom Austin recalled the feeling of excitement: 'Down on the beaches below could be seen signs of great preparations and we supplied several parties to haul guns up near our position.'[1] Rumours swept the trenches and flourished in the rest areas. By the last week of July Sergeant Cameron believed that the light horse might soon no longer be needed. Optimistically, he wrote: 'We are likely to go back to our horses as soon as Kitchener's army arrives. Horses! Oh how we will appreciate them after this rabbit warren.'[2]

The light horsemen's hopes that they would be sent back to Egypt were soon dashed. Instead of being released by the incoming troops, the 3rd Light Horse Brigade was destined to play a big role in the forthcoming offensive. One approach to Chunuk Bair was blocked by the Turks at The Nek and by row after row of well-developed and strongly held trenches on Baby 700. The main attack on Chunuk Bair, mostly entrusted to the New Zealanders, would have to come from another direction: up the wild gullies, where it was thought the Turks were few. The most important role given to the Australians, the capture of Hill 971, was entrusted to the 4th Infantry Brigade under Colonel John Monash. Once the New Zealanders were securely on Chunuk Bair the Australian Light Horse would launch a converging action across The Nek.

The 3rd Light Horse Brigade was ordered to attack the Turkish lines facing them. It was felt that the officers and men were already familiar with the sector, and they had not yet been involved in a heavy offensive action. So that the maximum pressure could be applied, there would also be assaults made by Chauvel's 1st Light Horse Brigade at Quinn's Post and Pope's Hill. These actions, set for 7 August, would be preceded by infantry attacks at Lone Pine and German Officers' Trench. The Lone Pine assault was to be a diversionary attack to draw the Turks' attention to the southern part of the Turks' line and would begin on the evening of the 6th. The attack on German Officers' Trench, set for midnight, was supposed to secure this part of the line and provide protection for the light horsemen's flank.

The main architect of this scheme was Brigadier General Andrew Skeen, Birdwood's chief staff officer. He met with Hughes and Antill on 1 August to outline their brigade's role. Skeen is an important but shadowy figure in the story of the Gallipoli campaign. He had Birdwood's full confidence and had been involved in all his main planning since the landing in April; until he was evacuated severely ill in September, he was the main hand in most of the staff work. He took no further part in the main theatres of the war but was able to resume a high-level career in the Indian army after the war. Sir Brudenell White, the Australian who replaced him, recalled that on Anzac he had been 'keen, clean shaven, eager face … and untiring – and at no time anything but the complete optimist'.[3]

Large numbers of British and Indian troops were now landing and more light horse reinforcements began to arrive on Russell's Top. Major Tom Redford, writing before the 8th Light Horse had received any orders, noted: 'We are expecting a big move forward by our side very shortly.'[4] Miell also knew to expect something and made a wager with Reynell that the regiment would be in Constantinople before Christmas.[5] Sergeant Cameron's reaction was more sober: 'We are nearing the day of great things now … we go forward in the full consciousness of a "duty" clear before us. God grant comfort to those in anxiety and sorrow and give our leaders wisdom.'[6]

After the conference with Skeen, Hughes and Antill made a perfunctory reconnaissance of the enemy's positions opposite. A fortnight earlier the brigade and regimental commanders had gone out on a destroyer to get a better view of the approaches to Baby 700. The appreciation prepared by the two officers failed to identify the full strength of the Turks' machine-gun positions, but still they could see the peril of any attack across The Nek. On 2 August Hughes and Antill discussed an outline plan with Godley. In this, and in the discussions with Skeen, both officers expressed their concern about the strength of the enemy facing them. They were reassured that the brigade would be heavily supported, directly and by other diversionary attacks, and that surprise, and the short distance to be crossed, would provide an essential advantage.[7] A weakness of the plan was that so many aspects relied on the success of others.

The forthcoming breakout was mainly entrusted to the troops of Godley's division. At the landing he had had the smaller force allocated a secondary role to Major General William Bridges's 1st Australian Division, but this had now been built up to virtually the size of the corps. Bridges had been killed by a sniper's bullet a few weeks after the landing and his division, having passed to Harold Walker, a British officer, now had the lesser role to perform.

Many officers found Godley civil and courteous. After a visit to the 8th Light Horse, Lieutenant Colonel White decided that 'he seems a decent bird'.[8] But he had none of the bonhomie which, though somewhat contrived, made Birdwood popular with the troops. He was unable to relate to the men on any personal level and made no attempt at it. On the other hand, his reputation as an administrator and trainer had already been firmly established. He was always alert, insisted on high standards of dress and conduct, and was rigid in his application of discipline. Antill, who bore similar authoritarian traits, described him as 'a forbidding sort of a man, but a good soldier'.[9]

Unlike peacetime exercises, war is a contest with shifting rules, and Godley was unable to see that behaviour which had been appropriate in the past might now be out of place. The military textbooks were no longer keeping pace with innovation and change. Godley failed to allow room for initiative and imagination when receiving and preparing orders, and it is clear that he accepted his instructions from Birdwood without question. Sadly, he lacked the wisdom that Sergeant Cameron prayed would be bestowed on the leaders in whose hands the light horsemen's lives now lay.

Godley's officers learned that he did not expect his directions to be questioned. Some months earlier, during exercises in Egypt, he had admonished one of them, saying: 'I particularly want you to understand that when I order your brigade to come into action in line of batteries, you have got to do it, even if you think it is impossible.'[10] The incident itself is not important, but his words do give an insight into his attitude.

Unfortunately, Godley was quite capable of ordering the impossible, and of expecting it to be done. A bold thrust of a pencil across a map is a lot different from an understrength assault into machine-gun fire, against entrenchments. After the repulse of the big Turkish attack on 19 May, Godley had ordered the New Zealanders to make a counter-attack in daylight across The Nek. They objected, Russell agreed, and the attack was cancelled. The light horse officers were probably aware that among the New Zealanders it was rumoured that Lieutenant Colonel Mackesy, the commanding officer of the Auckland Mounted Rifles, had been relieved of his command and returned to Egypt for having failed to make the attack.[11]

Reynell, already mentioned in despatches for his part in repulsing the

Turks in June, and now acting in command of the 9th Light Horse while Miell was away again in hospital at Lemnos, began to get ready for the upcoming battle. He wrote:

> We are going to make a big attack – our casualties are bound to be very heavy indeed as we shall have to cross a confined space under fire of a half circle of Turk trenches. However I have every confidence in our fellows and even if 75% of us are knocked out I believe the other 25% will get there. I am going to have a talk to them and prepare their minds for heavy losses and impress on them the necessity of getting there or dying in the attempt. However I believe they will behave well and do or die anyway. I see big stacks of new stretchers being made just near by our bivouac.[12]

By 4 August he had his instructions and was feeling more assured. Still, the possibility that he could be killed was not far from his mind and he addressed some thoughts to his wife and young son:

> Got first definite news about the attack. Our [brigade] is to take the trenches on the neck [sic] with good covering fire after a very heavy and prolonged bombardment and so it should present no difficulties. I am looking forward to the attack very much as I am very hopeful that it may result in a glorious stroke. Goodbye and may it be a consolation to you to realise that I have been some use here and Dickaboo must grow up quick and be a comfort to his Mother and Grandfather.[13]

Other men must have had similar thoughts. Tom Austin recalled: 'On the 4th we were issued with final orders. Throughout the whole day everyone was busy and as soon as the work was done most of us sat down to pen a word of fare-well home.'[14]

Sergeant Pinnock sent a letter to his family trying not to worry them, saying that they might not hear from him for a while. The next one he wrote was from a hospital bed in Egypt. He was able to report that he had survived: 'When I wrote … I felt convinced that it would be the last letter I would ever write. I could not say anything definite as we were told that any letters referring in any way to us making an advance would be destroyed.'[15]

The orders for the brigade's part in the attack, put together by Hughes and Antill, were lengthier and more detailed than many of those prepared on the peninsula, and one officer even complained about the length of time it took him to copy them down.[16] They set the time of the attack for 4.30 in the early morning of 7 August. Unfortunately, no matter how fully they were written, they could not overcome the impossibility of the task that had been set.

The actual assault was to be undertaken by the 8th and 10th regiments and would be made in four waves of 150 men each; the front was too narrow to allow for any more. The 9th Light Horse would be in reserve. There would also be two companies of the Royal Welch Fusiliers and a battalion of the Cheshire Regiment. Their application was not finalised until the day before the attack. The fusiliers were to share the same peril as the light horsemen by having to launch themselves across Monash Valley to tie the 1st and 3rd Light Horse Brigades' actions together.

For the venture to succeed it was necessary for the enemy to be taken by surprise, for no-man's-land to be crossed quickly, the front line captured and the enemy routed, and for the back trenches to be only lightly held. Once the assaulting waves had gone over they would have some protection from artillery and machine-gun fire when they were in the enemy trenches. They would be supported by machine-guns and rifles, while a heavy bombardment from ships and artillery would have 'softened up' the enemy by damaging his trenches, causing casualties, and supposedly reducing his will to fight.

It was intended that the first line, drawn entirely from the 8th Regiment, would attack the complex of trenches that extended across The Nek using just bombs and bayonets. The second line would pass through to take the first rows of trenches where they broadened out across the approach of the ridge. The third line – the first from the 10th Light Horse – would pursue the enemy, whom it was imagined would now be in full flight. A fourth line carried shovels and tools and would consolidate the gains.

By any stretch of the imagination, this was an ambitious plan. Some officers put aside their misgivings in the hope that it was audacious enough to succeed. The plan did not take into account the fact that the preliminary shelling by the artillery and the ships' guns would have removed the vital element of surprise, nor did it acknowledge the stoicism of the Turkish regiment directly opposing the Australians – the same one that had lost heavily in its own attack here a few weeks earlier. Nor could the plan adequately consider the location and strength of the enemy's machine-guns: it did identify five likely positions, but three of these were beyond the bounds set for the assaulting force. Although the orders were clear that the artillery fire would cease at 4.30 am, when the assault would commence, some of the brigade expected that there would be close artillery support throughout the action. The reliance on bombs and bayonets was unrealistic, although in the event it was not to matter much.

The men were ordered to charge without any rounds in their rifles. Firing while crossing the narrow no-man's-land was not practical, and it was normal practice – it was, for example, certainly the case at the landing in April – to have magazines charged but no round in the firing chamber. Loading was then a simple action of working the rifle's bolt. This may have been how the order was meant to be interpreted. In any case, the troops would be armed with little more than a bayonet, and some primitive bombs, when they came to grips with the enemy. Godley was proposing to use the light horsemen in a massed bayonet attack of a kind that had been rendered ineffective by developments in weaponry back at the time of the American Civil War. The dependence on bombs for offensive action on Gallipoli also proved unwise. It was discovered that an operation was brought to a standstill once bombs began being exchanged at close quarters. Against effectively employed modern machine-guns such tactics had no chance.

Antill claimed he was never convinced that the plan was a good one, but it is clear that once he had been given his instructions he was determined to see them carried out. His own written orders to the troop leaders make this clear, although we do not know if these are his own words or those relayed from Godley. He wrote emphatically:

One thing must be clearly understood and appreciated – WE ARE OUT TO STAY – THERE IS NO COMING BACK – the surest means are DASH and DETERMINATION. No time to waste on prisoners – no notice of tricks of the enemy such as 'cease fire' and there is no RETIRE. ONCE OUT OF OUR TRENCHES – OUT FOR GOOD and the assault, once for all goes right home.[17]

He gave his verbal orders in a similar tone. Lieutenant Wilfred Robinson of the 8th Light Horse later recalled with some resentment that 'our BM talked volubly about getting over "with rifle butts and pick handles" and chasing the other fellow out'.[18]

Although they may have been anxious, most of the men expected the assault to be a success. The brigade's victory in repulsing the Turkish attack a few weeks earlier had fed their self-confidence. Clearly few reflected on the fact that they would now be taking the place of the unfortunate Turkish infantry who had tried to cross the same space under similar perilous conditions.

A couple of months earlier Trooper Alex Borthwick had expressed his fear that the 8th Light Horse would never see action. His brother, Keith, was an officer in the regiment. Now, as the time for battle approached, he wrote a few words home:

> I hope Keith and I pull through all right but if we don't you will know we have done our little bit. Poor old Mother must not worry too much, and I hope, if we should have the bad luck to get hit today, that Father will console both of you by remembering that we quitted ourselves like men.[19]

Because the weather was getting hot the men's woollen tunic coats had been taken from them a few days earlier, leaving them with only hats or sun helmets, woollen shirts, breeches or shorts, and boots. It had been a stupid idea and it caused great discomfort. Certainly the days were hot, but the evenings were cold, so the troops shivered in the trenches at night. The light horsemen would have to attack in their 'shirt-sleeve' order, carrying their ammunition in the infantry webbing pouches that had only recently been issued to replace their leather bandoliers. They would also carry a full water bottle, six biscuits and a field dressing (bandage roll) pinned inside their shirts. Some men were detailed to carry planks or ladders, extra bombs, sandbags, wire-cutters, picks, shovels or periscopes. Trooper Meldrum wrote:

> On Thursday 5th we got orders to pack up our spare belongings and get ready. We started by sewing white patches on our shirts; one on the back and on each sleeve. Our bundles were thrown into big heaps on the edge of the cliffs and we were issued with our rations for 48 hours. At 8 O'clock we went round to secret saps and here waited, about 40 yards from the Turks. We sat in our saps and trenches all night and shivered. I can't say we slept – any rate I didn't.[20]

Lieutenant Colonel Miell was able to return to his regiment in time to resume command, and several other men contrived to get back from the hospitals to be with their squadrons. Captain Vernon Piesse of the 10th Regiment was one of these, arriving on the evening before the attack. 'I'd never have been able to stand up again if I hadn't,' he told the others.[21] There were some who should have been sent away but who hung on to be with their mates. Sergeant Gollan was very ill but he successfully pleaded with the doctor to be allowed to remain.[22] Corporal Arthur Tetley was urged by the doctor to go out. Some weeks earlier some shells had burst in front of him, knocking him about, and his nerves were badly affected. But he was devoted to his troop members and insisted on staying.[23]

Many of the light horsemen on Pope's Hill and Russell's Top watched the fighting over at Lone Pine during the afternoon of 6 August; it was like some overture to their own forthcoming battle. Here, at 5.30 pm, the infantrymen of the 1st Australian Brigade launched a blow that was hoped to draw in the Turks' reserves and prevent them from reinforcing the places where the next main attacks were to be made. For two hours wave after wave could be seen crossing into the Turkish lines. The noise told the distant onlookers that the fighting was heavy. For the rest of the night the sound of machine-gun bursts and rifle fire continued while, at regular intervals, shells came across exploding on the Turks' lines beyond The Nek. Sergeant Nugent recalled: 'We had to sit in trenches all night [and] heard other attacks around us. All night we sat, and the strain was awful. About 2 am I went to sleep and slept for about an hour. About 3 am rum was served out.'[24]

William McGrath, another of the 8th Light Horse's sergeants, later wrote:

B Squadron manned [the] trenches ... all day and night. Relieved for meals one troop at a time. Major Redford and Mr Henty more serious than other officers and seemed to realise the gravity of operations more than the juniors. All were in good and bright spirits and so confident. Major [Redford] gave me several instructions but did not speak as if he expected the end and gave no instructions re disposal of any of his property. [Sergeant Major] C.H. Cameron was very sober and gave me a letter to post as did several of the men. Apart from that each man either took all his valuables or had them packed in his kit. All kits were stacked at entrance of Todd Road, Broadway.

A double issue of rum was given to each troop and as the night was
very cold was found most acceptable.[25]

The success of the infantry at Lone Pine, despite heavy losses, inspired
the light horsemen. What they could not yet know was that the further
attack at German Officers' Trench, which was to remove the machine-guns
enfilading the light horsemen's positions, had failed. The movement on Hill
971 was also breaking down.

At 4 am the artillery, which had been firing through the night, began
to concentrate on the Turks opposite Russell's Top. At the same time the
warships added their weight, although this contribution has usually been
overestimated: most of the gunfire was provided by just one destroyer.
The use of an intense artillery shelling as a preliminary to an attack was a
tactic in use on the Western Front. However, at Anzac it was not possible to
provide the same concentrated barrages used in France and Belgium and,
although the shelling at The Nek was 'intense' by Gallipoli standards, the
damage inflicted on the enemy was later considered to be disappointing. As
the moment for the attack neared, the men of the 8th Light Horse in the first
line prepared to spring forth.

The Australians' front trench, from which they would attack, ran in a
rough line, north to south, for approximately 150 metres, ending at both
sides in cliff edges. Only half of this line was in direct sight of the enemy;
the northern half was concealed in dead ground. This hidden line was
actually a secret sap which had been made without parapet or parados and
was partly overhung by low scrub. On the right the ground was relatively
flat, but in front of the secret sap it rose up and this slope provided some
protection for the attackers.

For the assault the first line was split into two parts. On the right, in the
deep trench and the saps stretching forward from it, about 75 men stood on
the firestep or at the entrances to the saps, with a similar number of men of
the second line standing behind them. On the left, in the secret sap, there
was not room enough for the 150 men of the two waves. The first line had
to lie in front of the sap in dead ground, while the second line crouched in
the sap behind them.

The first wave was made up of all the available men of Redford's
B Squadron, together with a couple of troops from A Squadron. The troop
leaders were Lieutenants Wilson, Marsh, Talbot Woods, the youthful
Lieutenant Anderson, and Sergeant Grenfell, and Lieutenants Borthwick

and Henty, the last named having recently returned from hospital. The 10th Light Horse was in the support trenches ready to take the place of the departing men once the attack was underway.

The new medical officer of the 8th Light Horse, Captain Francis Beamish, was preparing for a busy morning. He knew that the casualties would be heavy. Observing the troops, he noted that 'before the time came [they] heaped up pocket books and keepsakes that were to be sent home'.[26]

The brigade headquarters had already moved from the shelters on the rear cliff edges to a forward dug-out to be in closer touch with the assaulting regiments. Carew Reynell and another officer of the 9th Regiment were detached to marshal and guide the assaulting troops to their positions.

As zero hour approached it became known that the assault on German Officer's Trench had failed, that Monash's brigade was nowhere near its objective and that the New Zealanders had made unnecessary halts, leaving them well short of Chunuk Bair and hence not in place to be able to threaten the enemy from the rear. Birdwood could see that things were beginning to slip through his fingers but decided that the plan had to be followed anyway. The light horsemen would be very vulnerable but, if Godley threw them in now, it might make things easier for the New Zealanders and possibly they could still take the hill. In a crucial decision, made in the knowledge that the 3rd Light Horse Brigade would now be virtually unsupported, Birdwood decided to allow their attack to proceed.

The brigade headquarters was connected to the division by telephone. The lines provided the staff with limited communication but not the direct control that would come later with more advanced technology. Antill contacted the division to ask whether he was still to go ahead. 'The laconic reply,' he later said, 'was that the attack must proceed according to plan.'[27] Lieutenant Colonel Alexander White was at the headquarters with Dale, the young Duntroon officer who had been made adjutant after Crowl had been killed, when the reply was received. Although he felt very anxious about the situation, White had decided that he would lead his regiment in the attack. Antill later described this moment:

White heard the divisional final order, and in reply to a suggestion that he should best superintend the advance in rear, he said that as he was in charge of the business, he elected to decide his own position. He then shook hands and said goodbye to the brigadier and brigade major.[28]

White and Dale went up to the front trench and quickly took up their positions. In shirt sleeves and sun helmet, White was almost indistinguishable from the men. It was noticed that 'he had no coat on and round his neck wore a chain and locket with his young wife and infant baby's photo'.[29] The men were waiting, each with his own thoughts, pressed against the trench sides, gripping their rifles with bayonets fixed, listening for the signal to go. White watched the hands of his watch tick towards 'zero'.

CHAPTER 10

'Come on boys.
Come on. Come on.'

As 4.30 am, the appointed time for the attack, approached, the men on Russell's Top, Pope's Hill and Quinn's Post stood waiting in the dim light for the simple orders that would launch them against the enemy's earthen fortifications. Further along the ridge, up around Chunuk Bair, the grand plan was beginning to fall apart with the New Zealanders unable to get into position to make their final assault on the heights.

All through the early hours of the morning, shells had been falling at intervals on the Turkish lines. One misdirected round crashed onto the Australians' parapet, close to the brigade's temporary headquarters. It took a few moments for composure to be regained, and Antill moved deeper into the dug-out for safety.

Sergeant Pinnock, who was waiting as part of the first line, later recalled: 'The warships had been pounding their trenches with heavy guns. They kept it up for two hours. It was simply one continual roar and nerve racking in the extreme. You can't for a moment imagine the awful din of exploding shells, it was really awful.'[1]

Just as the watches on Russell's Top reached 4.23 am, and the artillery shelling was expected to reach a crescendo, the firing ceased, 'cut short as if by a knife'.[2] White and Dale were standing with Major Redford and Lieutenant Robinson. Robinson, who would be the only one in the group to survive the next several minutes, recalled:

For a few moments no one spoke. Then the Colonel said: 'Come along Dale', and I remarked to Redford: 'What do you make of it?

There is seven minutes to go.' He replied: 'They may give them a heavy burst to finish.' For three minutes hardly a shot came from the Turks and then a scattered rifle fire broke out, above which could be heard distinctly the rattle of about 10 shots as each Turk machine-gun was made ready for action. I got my men ready and shook hands with Major Redford.[3]

This pause of several minutes erased any last hope that the enemy could be taken by surprise. They were now waiting for signs of movement from the Australians. When Captain George Hore, who was in the second line, wrote later to his mother, he confirmed the failure of the timings.

At 4 am we stood to arms in our trenches. In 25 minutes [the bombardment] stopped. Immediately a fierce crackle of fire came out of the Turkish trenches. We knew we were doomed. At 23 minutes past 4 we stood up on the banquettes of our trenches, and in a few minutes the crackle of musketry turned into an awful roar. Never have I heard such an awful sound and no wonder.[4]

The critical pause was not apparent to everyone. Some survivors' accounts make no mention of it at all, although the recollections of others are quite clear. Kent Hughes wrote to the official historian after the war: 'As far as I remember the bombardment did stop early, but at a time when seconds are minutes and minutes seem like hours I should hardly like to hazard a guess at the length of the period.'[5]

The men of the first wave put their feet onto pegs or in niches cut in the trench wall, others in front of the long sap gripped their rifles, while those in the shallow saps crouched ready to scramble out. Then on the order from White – 'Go!' – they climbed up, with their colonel at the lead. The moment they rose above ground level the rifle and machine-gun fire erupted as a roar sweeping through the Australians' ranks.

The historian Charles Bean wrote:

I shall never forget that moment. I was making my way along a path from the left of the area and was passing not very far away when [the] tremendous fusillade broke out. It rose from a fierce crackle into a roar in which you could distinguish neither rifle nor

George Lambert, *The charge of the 3rd Light Horse Brigade at The Nek, 7 August 1915*. (AWM ART07965)

Above Major Tom Todd leads a parade of the 10th Light Horse Regiment before departing for the war. Instead of acting in a mounted role, the regiment served in the trenches alongside the infantry on Gallipoli. (AWM P09573.005)

Below left Colonel Frederic Hughes who commanded the 3rd Light Horse Brigade during the charge at The Nek. This formal portrait was taken before the brigade left Australia. (AWM H19195)

Below right Lieutenant Colonel Noel Brazier, commanding officer of the 10th Light Horse Regiment. He is in the uniform of the regiment he commanded before the war. Brazier tried unsuccessfully to have the charge at The Nek stopped. (AWM P0783/01)

Above left Lieutenant Colonel Alexander White, of the 8th Light Horse Regiment, with his wife and infant son, shortly after his appointment to command the regiment. He died leading his men at The Nek. (Mrs M. McPherson)

Above right Lieutenant Colonel Jack Antill was the Brigade Major of the 3rd Light Horse Brigade at the charge at The Nek. He was later promoted to command the brigade. (AWM G01330)

Right Officers of C Squadron, 8th Light Horse Regiment, in camp at Broadmeadows. All took part in the charge at The Nek. (L to R) Captain A. McLaurin (wounded), Major A. Deeble, Lieutenant C. Dale (killed), Second Lieutenant W. Robinson (wounded), and Second Lieutenant C. Carthew (killed). Only Deeble survived the action uninjured. (AWM DAX0181)

Recently arrived at Anzac, some of B Squadron of the 8th Light Horse Regiment are gathered in a rest area behind the front line. They were soon to man the trenches at The Nek. (AWM H03164)

Above Central characters in The Nek drama on the slopes of Walker's Ridge, near the 3rd Light Horse Brigade's headquarters. The divisional commander, General Godley (left), is speaking to Colonel Hughes (centre, light jacket) and Lieutenant Colonel Antill (right). (AWM J02715)

Right Light horsemen in the trenches at The Nek. Trench warfare was dramatically different from the mounted operations the light horse expected when they enlisted. (AWM J02719)

In the trenches on Gallipoli, Major Thomas Redford observes the enemy lines using a periscope. He was later killed in the 8th Light Horse's charge on 7 August 1915. (AWM H03124)

A crew of the 9th Light Horse Regiment manning the machine-gun at Turk's Point. This gun fired on the Turks across The Nek during the attack on 7 August 1915. (AWM J02704)

Signaller James Campbell of the 8th Light Horse Regiment, in his dugout burrowed into the rear slopes of Walker's Ridge at Anzac. (AWM H03197)

Captain Phil Fry of the 10th Light Horse Regiment in the trenches at The Nek. The popular officer survived the charge on 7 August but was killed at Hill 60 three weeks later. (AWM A05401)

The last living survivor of the charge at The Nek, Lionel Simpson DCM, died in 1991 aged 100. In 1984 he visited George Lambert's famous painting of the action. (Author)

Sunday crowds in Melbourne outside *The Argus* newspaper office anxiously await further reports of the fighting on Gallipoli, and the inevitable accompanying long list of casualties. (AWM H11613)

machine-gun, but just one continuous roaring tempest. One could not help an involuntary shiver: God help anyone that was out in that tornado.[6]

Over 150 Australians in no-man's-land seemed to go limp and then drop like rag dolls. It was 'as though their limbs had become strings,' said one observer at Pope's Hill.[7] Others, whose bodies were struck by bombs or machine-gun bursts, were thrown violently about. The more fortunate were immediately wounded and fell back into their trenches.

Sergeant Pinnock records:

We all got over and cheered, but they were waiting ready for us and simply gave us a solid wall of lead. We did not get ten yards. Everyone fell like lumps of meat. I got mine shortly after I got over the bank, and it felt like a million ton hammer falling on my shoulder. However I managed to crawl back.[8]

The terrible sound of the Turks' fire became an enduring memory of every survivor in the 8th Light Horse. Each enemy soldier sighting down his rifle must have squeezed his trigger as soon as the Australians burst into view. The machine-guns sustained their fire, while the riflemen reloaded with mechanical speed, firing again and again.

Lieutenant Eliot Wilson, who commanded B Squadron's D Troop, was in the forefront of the charge. He was out waving his revolver, calling 'Now then boys', when he was shot. He managed to stagger on until a bomb exploded alongside him and he fell. One witness said there was an explosion under his body, probably from his own revolver. Major Redford died close by.

A sergeant wrote:

Our gallant major, whilst lying facing the enemy's trench (10 yards away) in the front of his men received a bullet through his brain as he raised his head slightly to observe. He died with a soft sigh and laid his head gently on his hands as if tired. A braver and more honourable man never donned uniform.[9]

Within several seconds almost every officer in the first wave was hit; there was not to be a single survivor from among them. One troop had been led out by a sergeant, 23-year-old Clifton Grenfell. He was killed instantly. The torrent of metal tore through the ranks, cutting them down in swathes.

Trooper Jack Dale was one who was able to reach some sheltered ground:

> Those of us that got over the very slight rise of ground were simply mown down. I was one of three who were carrying a big plank which we had to throw over any entanglements, and then the trenches when we got there. We got pretty close, and were lucky to get behind a slight rise in the ground. We had to lie flat on our stomachs. We were pretty safe from the bullets [and] started to dig ourselves in, as it would have been madness and certain death to charge against such a fire. Wounded fellows were crawling past us, some with terrible wounds caused by bombs. All you could do was to make way and help them past.[10]

Another trooper carrying one of the planks was Lionel Simpson. Interviewed in 1984, this decorated old soldier, a holder of the Distinguished Conduct Medal, then in his mid-nineties, was the last known living survivor of the charge. He recalled running forward until he felt the man on the other end holding back. He looked behind to see that his comrade had been wounded. In an instant he too was hit, in the head and the shoulder, and fell to the ground. He remembered feeling 'disgusted' when he heard some of the survivors calling to others to fall back. Simpson was one of Wilson's troop, and last saw his leader running forward waving his revolver, yelling 'Come on boys. Come on. Come on.'[11]

The assault on The Nek was to coincide with similar efforts on Pope's Hill and Quinn's Post, and with the big attack on Chunuk Bair. At Pope's Hill two squadrons of the 1st Light Horse Regiment, which were temporarily commanded by Major William Glasgow – a man of powerful personality who would rise to high command by the end of the war – faced the Turks across a gully. It was planned that one part of this force would get down into the deep sheltered end of the gully and make its rush from there. The assault by the two squadrons would be coordinated with movements on The Nek. The confusion over timings on Russell's Top did not matter as much as it might have, because the Turks detected movement and the 1st

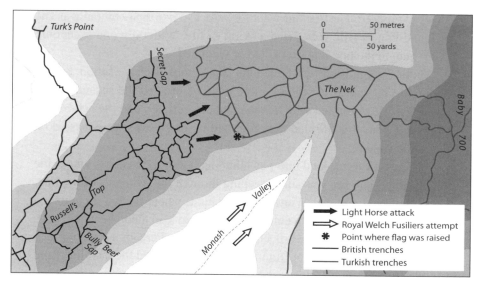

The opposing trenches at The Nek.

Light Horse had to make its assault prematurely. The New South Welshmen went into heavy Turkish fire and launched themselves upon the enemy with bayonets and bombs. They managed to get well into the trenches, fighting desperately, while their losses mounted rapidly. They were holding on, fighting wild bombing duels, as the attack on The Nek reached a climax.

At Quinn's Post the attackers were from the 2nd Light Horse Regiment and they well knew that their task would be madness under normal circumstances. They had been reassured by the same promises that had been given to the 3rd Light Horse Brigade. They were told that the capture of German Officers' Trench would remove the threat of enfilading fire from their right, the New Zealanders would have captured Chunuk Bair and be moving down on the enemy's rear, and the artillery would have provided a devastating preliminary bombardment. As dawn approached, the Queenslanders saw that the artillery shelling had had very little effect, and that Chunuk Bair and German Officers' Trench were still held by the enemy.

As with The Nek, the attack at Quinn's Post would be undertaken by four waves of troops, but here each wave would have only 50 men. Colonel Harry Chauvel, the most competent of the light horse brigade commanders who within a few years would lead the Desert Mounted Corps, allowed the attack to proceed. The first line went forward, and like their comrades at The Nek and Pope's Hill, they faced a storm of fire. With only one exception, every man in the first line was killed or wounded.

Major George Bourne, who led the attack, took decisive action. Seeing nothing to be gained in sending more men, he ordered the second line to stand fast. He consulted with his commanding officer, and the action was stopped. Chauvel confirmed the order and no more lives were wasted on this futile venture.

At The Nek the second line was climbing out of the trenches while rifle and machine-gun fire was still sweeping through the remnants of the first. Had Lieutenant Colonel White stayed behind, where he could command his squadrons, rather than deciding that he had to lead them, he would have seen the destruction of half of his fine regiment. Perhaps he would then have acted as Bourne had at Quinn's Post and prevented the next line from leaving. But White was dead, and Major Arthur Deeble, who commanded the second wave, took no restraining action. The attack proceeded under its own momentum and, moments after the first line went over, the second followed.

On the right half of the line, which was the most exposed, four troops scrambled out of the trench. George Grant, a New Zealand-born lieutenant, had just arrived at Anzac, having left Melbourne in early May with the regiment's fifth batch of reinforcements. The troop he led out at The Nek was quickly shot down, and Grant fell in a pile of men. He lay dead with three others, on top of an unconscious Trooper White, who later struggled free and got to safety. Lieutenants Thomas Howard and Charles Carthew, and most of their men, were killed at the same time. Of all the officers in his group, only Captain George Hore survived to go any appreciable distance. He was later able to get back and received some treatment before he was sent off to hospital. Hore left this record:

We saw our fate in front of us, but we were pledged to go and, to their eternal credit, the word being given, not a man in the second line stayed in his trench. As I jumped out I looked down the line, and they were all rising over the parapet. We bent low, and ran as hard as we could. Ahead we could see the trench aflame with rifle-fire. All round were smoke and dust kicked up by the bullets. I felt a sting on my shoulder. I passed our first line, all dead or dying it seemed, and went on a bit further, and flung myself down about 40 yards from the Turkish trenches. I was a bit ahead of my men, having got a good start and travelled lighter. I looked around and saw them all down mostly hit. I did not know what to do. I was protected by a little – a very little fold in the ground and by a dead Turk – dead about six weeks.[12]

Doug Bethune, a South African War veteran, was a temporary sergeant who was killed in the first line. His younger brother, Norman, also to die later in the war, was in the second line and for a brief while was caught up among the men falling back from the initial charge. He survived to give an account:

The order was given just about daybreak … and the first line (in which Doug's troop was first) went out. Numbers were shot almost as soon as they got out of our saps and few if any reached the Turkish trenches. Some of the second line (of which my troop was part) just got out and that was all when the few that were left got orders to retire and came back onto us, in fact before a lot of us were able to get out they came back into the narrow saps in which we had been waiting. It was a nasty thing altogether and nothing was gained.[13]

Back among the 9th Light Horse, Sergeant Cameron was able to see what was happening.

We saw them climb out and move forward about ten yards and lie flat. The second line did likewise … as they rose to charge the Turkish Machine-Guns just poured out lead and our fellows went down like corn before the scythe. The distance to the enemy trench was less than 50 yards yet not one of those two lines got anywhere near it.[14]

So intense was the fire that nowhere was safe. Lieutenant Colonel Miell, who had gone up to an observation position, looked over the parapet to watch the progress. He was shot through the head and killed. This meant that two of the brigade's regimental commanders were now dead.

On the left of the line there was some slight depression in front of the long forward sap. Even so, Lieutenant Robinson, an officer described by one of his men as 'a big old cocky, [and] a good man',[15] was immediately hit as he rose:

> As I climbed out of the 'secret sap' on the extreme left, my hand was
> shattered and I was almost knocked senseless by a bursting shell or
> a bomb. By some means, either falling or struggling frantically I got
> back in to the sap, where I remember trying to think what happened
> and suddenly becoming aware of a terrific rifle fire and later was
> fully restored to my senses by a lot of men unceremoniously walking
> over me.[16]

Robinson's troop sergeant was Charles Lyons, who takes up the story from
this point in his account: 'Our officer was shot through the hand. I was left
in charge and being unable to jam past the men, jumped up and ran round
to the front of the sap, calling on the men to follow, but just as I got out, the
1st line fell back nearly all wounded.'[17]

Some of the survivors were now calling for everyone to fall back. Lyon
saw his corporal, Arthur Tetley, lying seriously wounded and he and some
others managed to drag him back as they withdrew. '[We] laid him on the
bottom of the trench,' Lyon wrote. 'His leg was in a fearful state, a machine-
gun had got on to him, but he stood it wonderfully and a 10th man applied
first aid. The stretcher-bearers were fearfully busy, and he had to lie there
over two hours before it was possible to get him away.'[18] The farmer from
faraway King Island died on the hospital ship next day.

Once out of the trench, and seeing the futility of their task, Major Deeble
and Lieutenant Higgins had sought some cover. Deeble found himself well
out in front and without a mark on him:

> My own line came under a most deadly hail of machine-gun, bomb,
> and rifle fire, and the men fell all around me. No man hesitated, yet
> I had none to carry further. I fell on my face, and, taking the cover
> of the nearest depression in the ground managed to get together, or
> rather, speak to about 8 or 10 men not yet shot. I determined to wait
> for the 3rd line and sweep on with them. [The] 2nd line got as far
> forward as the first, I must have been the only officer in the line
> except Lieutenant Higgins, whose few followers were some distance
> to my left.[19]

Lieutenant Andy Crawford had run forward until he was hit. He recalled:

> I only got about fifteen or twenty yards. I could see the Turks two

deep in their trench. I could see one soldier firing over another chap's shoulder. A bullet hit me [in the hip] and spun me around. Bowled me over like a rabbit. I lay there and couldn't move and another bullet went through the fleshy part of my back. Four or five blokes came out and pulled me back.[20]

The last officer still left standing was Major McLaurin, who was in command on the left. He had led a counter-attack to drive the enemy out of these trenches only a few weeks before, shooting three Turks with his revolver. Now, leaving his trench, he had run forward about 25 metres, still partly protected by the small dip. Reaching the top of the rise, he saw that there was nobody left in front of him. In that same instant he noticed Lieutenant Leo Anderson, the young Duntroon officer, lying in a hole partly covered by some bushes; he had been mortally wounded. McLaurin threw himself down and set about trying to drag the young man back to safe ground. While doing this he was wounded in the face, a round or some shrapnel striking him across the bridge of his nose. A brave teenager, Leslie Lawry, who had joined the regiment as one of its trumpeters, took over and pulled the dying Anderson in.

Troopers Meldrum, Boyton and McConnan were among those who, after being hit, were able to get back to safety. Only from the few such survivors do we learn of what was happening to the unfortunate men trapped in front of the Turkish fire. Meldrum recalled:

We had not covered half the distance before we met a wall of lead from machine-guns, rifles and bombs. Our first line propped and dropped. By the time the trench was reached you could count the men on your fingers. We were about half-way by this time, and had lost heavily, so we pulled our line together, and rushed forward. I got about five yards when I felt a bullet go through my hat, and it knocked me out. I seemed to be there a terribly long time, but it could have only been a few seconds. I heard our chaps still cheering as they charged so I jumped up and went on again. I got about 10 yards then another bullet took a piece of skin off my right eye. I dropped down again, as there didn't seem to be any of our chaps left.[21]

Walter McConnan made light of his injuries in a letter home:

My crack is really nothing only a graze on the back from a piece of red hot bomb or shrapnel. It is a bit sore but scratches do not count here and after all I was most lucky to get let down with it. I was out in the open getting along on my hands and knees at the time and when bowled over managed to roll into one of our saps to safety. While waiting about the dressing station I went about the stretchers helping where I could. I found young Sanderson of Benalla with a shattered leg. He was patient and brave. Australians can die I can tell you.[22]

Trooper Vernon Boyton had seen the first line shot down in front of him. Despite his serious wounds he survived, but took no further active part in the war. He wrote to his sister:

Well, they were all mown down except one or two who staggered back wounded. Then our turn came, and we made a dash for it. We had to trample over the dead bodies of our first line. I got within about six yards of their trench when I seemed to be hit everywhere through my right leg, my right forearm, my right hand, the first finger of which was hanging off and blood pouring everywhere.[23]

Once out of the trenches the men of the second line saw only a few of their comrades still struggling forward. The rest lay dead or wounded, or had scrambled for shelter in the shallow holes or in the slight dip in front of the long sap. Dozens of men were frightfully injured and were to lie out in front beyond help until death slowly overtook them. Others, thrashing about, making dashes for safety, or trying to crawl back, were hit repeatedly. The more fortunate hugged the ground while rounds passed only centimetres above them.

CHAPTER 11

The Decision

Several lines of machine-gun fire converged on the short strip of ground over which the two attacking waves of Victorian light horsemen had tried to pass. Added to this were the cracking fusillades of rifle fire from the Turks' front line, and from the tiers of trenches that rose up the slopes of Baby 700. Those men who had taken cover may have been safe from the bullets but they were still exposed to bombs being thrown over.

The distance between the opposing trenches was reckoned to be about 40 metres. Since these were not parallel lines, the gap was greater at some points but smaller near the centre. The land between was rough and broken. The Australians had to charge up a slope over ground covered in parts by thick low scrub, in some places stripped by machine-gun fire or burnt by flares, and concealing dips and holes and an old sunken gravel track. Fortunately, it did provide a couple of places of shelter for those few men whom fate allowed to escape the hail of bullets.

The continuous machine-gun and rifle fire chopped through the scrub, shaking the bushes and throwing up dust and stones. Bullets ripped and tore through the men. Not only were the living hit, but the dead also, including the rotting corpses of those from earlier fighting. Tom Austin records that 'the air reeked with the smell of cordite and the stench of dried Turkish victims left here since the attack on the 29th of June'.[1] When the last man of the second line dropped, the firing gradually slackened like a passing squall. The 10th Light Horse, making up the third and fourth lines, now filed into the front trenches and saps.

In the trenches there was chaos and confusion. It was not clear to those on Russell's Top exactly what was happening, although the concentration of heavy fire mounted against them was obvious. The front line was choked with the dead and wounded who had fallen back into the trenches. There were others dropping over the parapet, or into the shallow saps, who had crawled back desperately seeking safety. A few men were dragged in by comrades. So deadly was the fire that it was not safe even to peer above the top of the trenches.

The brigade headquarters had placed some observers to report on progress throughout the attack. While the second wave was out, Antill was advised that a small yellow and red marker flag had been seen. It flew for only a couple of minutes, then it was torn down. Perhaps it was the act of an individual who had ignored everything around him, and with a single-minded determination, carried the flag and stuck it defiantly in the enemy's parapet before being killed. But the flag could also indicate that part of the enemy line had been taken and that there were men there fighting desperately, holding on, and waiting for support. How should this sign be interpreted?

Lieutenant William Oliver later told the official historian: 'I am in a position to absolutely confirm the suggestion that a red and yellow flag was raised. It was my duty on that day to watch carefully for those flags as I was to hurry our trench mortars across as soon as the Turks had been driven out.'[2] Oliver said that he felt 'very nearly certain' that the flag was planted by Sergeant Roger Palmer. Others have suggested it was a Sergeant Cameron, or Trooper Grant. Geoffrey Grant was a lanky 19-year-old and his parents' only son. He had previously served in the army cadets and been an active boy scout and a good amateur athlete.

The orders for the attack stated that the captured trenches were to be marked by the small red-and-yellow flags such as were already widely used on Gallipoli as a means of identifying 'friendly' trenches to distant observers. They were carried by four men in each line. In a letter of sympathy to Grant's mother, his sergeant, Albert Pearce, reported that '[Grant] carried his signalling flags, though wounded, right to the Turkish trench'.[3]

Whether or not it was Grant or one of the others, the gallant soldier could not have anticipated that his determined act with his flags would send his comrades forward to their deaths. When Antill heard that the flag had been seen, he gave the order for the attack to continue, sending the Royal Welch Fusiliers, now waiting in Monash Valley, to make their assault on the trenches between The Nek and Pope's Hill.

While the 10th Light Horse was taking up its position, ready to continue the assault, the commanding officer, Noel Brazier, went to No. 8 Sap, in front of, and not far from, the brigade headquarters dug-out. Knowing it was too dangerous to raise his head, he used a periscope to look out on the battlefield. It was quickly apparent to him that the two previous waves had totally failed. All he could see were men lying prone and most of these seemed bloodied and still.

It was now Brazier's task to signal each of the two lines of his regiment forward. He had no vainglorious notions of leading his regiment in the attack, nor did anyone think that the commanding officers should. The timings were to be indicated by officers from the headquarters. Two or three officers had been assigned to this work: one was Bill Kent Hughes, the other, Kenneth McKenzie, a young Duntroon officer who had come over with the 9th Light Horse.

Brazier was greatly troubled by what he had seen of the destruction of the Victorians' two lines and could not give the order. A young staff officer rushed up to ask why he had not sent the waiting line. He replied that he would not do this without first seeking confirmation, or cancellation, of his orders. The progress of the attack lay in the balance. One of the 10th Regiment's corporals later recalled: 'It was a nerve-racking time waiting there for orders to go out, while the 8th Light Horse wounded dragged themselves back past us.'[4]

It was fully daylight as Brazier pushed his way back down the lines of trenches to the temporary brigade headquarters. There he found Antill and told him of the futility of continuing. Antill replied that a flag had been seen on the Turks' parapet and the attack must proceed. Brazier said that he had not been able to see a flag or any sign to indicate that a trench had been taken.

At this crucial moment there was a total absence of communication. The antagonism between these two men was in no way reduced by the gravity of the situation. Antill was furious at the impertinence of this troublesome and argumentative officer who had left his post to query orders which had so firmly been given. Brazier claimed that Antill responded to his appeal by roaring, 'Push on'! He then had to return to the front line where he gravely announced: 'I am sorry lads but the order is to go.'[5]

A small group, containing several of the best known men in the regiment, had gathered near a junction of the trenches waiting for Brazier to return with their orders. There was some expectation that the further assault would have to be cancelled. When they heard his news, Captain Piesse, Lieutenants Turnbull and Kidd, Captain Rowan, Sergeants Sanderson and

MacBean, and Sergeant Major Springall solemnly shook hands and said goodbye to each other. Then they quietly took their places with their men. Each man was resigned to his fate, determined only that he should not fail in his duty.

The word spread along the line. Trooper Harold Rush, a young farmhand, realising he was likely to die in the next few moments, turned to his mate beside him and said: 'Goodbye cobber. God bless you.'[6] Later, when his grieving parents were told this, they arranged for his last words to be inscribed on his headstone, which today lies in the cemetery on Walker's Ridge, a short distance from where he fell.

Major Tom Kidd, who was in command of the third line, steadied himself, gripped his revolver, then gave the order and led out the next wave. Once again a furious fire erupted from the Turks opposite and the Western Australians' attack was torn away. The roar and the smoke of the rifle and machine-gun fire had been joined by a Turkish 75-millimetre field gun bursting shrapnel low over no-man's-land.

It was proper for Brazier to have referred the situation back to head-quarters. Similar action, as we have seen, resulted in the attack at Quinn's Post being abandoned and many lives saved. Unfortunately, the response here had been quite different.

Hughes had not been at the temporary headquarters when Brazier went there. Early on he had gone up to a bombing emplacement close to the front line to see for himself what was happening. As a sportsman Hughes had the reputation as a 'stayer', someone 'who would shut his teeth and fight out the hardest race without once slacking'.[7] When Antill was approached to stop the attack, he felt no need to consult with the brigade commander to consider this possibility.

Although Antill claimed that the sighting of a marker flag demanded that the attack continue, he appears to have taken no action to learn whether more flags were now flying or, indeed, whether the single flag was still there. After the war he claimed that he 'immediately' advised divisional headquarters of the 'hopelessness of it all', but in the same sentence admits that this was not done until the attack finished.[8]

Major Love made an effort to find out what had happened to the Western Australians. He crawled out in front of a sap, where there was some protection, to see what could be done. He found Deeble of the 8th Regiment lying not far away, unable to move, and spoke briefly to him. Both officers agreed that it was quite impossible to advance against such firepower. Almost everyone else seemed to be dead or wounded, so he made his way back.

After leading the second line out, Deeble had sought some protection, where he waited hoping to join the following line of Western Australians as it came across. He later reported:

> This line scarcely left our trench before being broken, and the few men with me managed to dash a yard or two forward before falling down. I threw myself again on the ground. Seeing one or two to my left whom I could make hear me, and who were the few alive, I told them to scratch a little cover.[9]

The sun was rising, and in the morning light the men still fighting desperately on Pope's Hill saw the third line at The Nek shot away. The Royal Welch Fusiliers, fighting nearby, were seen to suffer a similar fate. The New South Welshmen at Pope's Hill now knew that their struggle could not be supported on either flank. Seeing their position was without hope and that many of the men were dead or wounded, they finally made a difficult withdrawal. Two hundred men had taken part; 154 were casualties.

Back among the light horsemen in the trenches on Russell's Top, the left of the line had become so choked with dead and wounded, and men trying to get back to safety or to receive treatment, that movement was difficult. Henry Foss would survive this day only to be killed, like his two brothers, later in the war. He was in a group in the trenches who found they could not get into position.

> My troop sat down in a fire trench waiting for orders, while D Troop of A Squadron filed past us. They halted for a while … I spoke to Gres Harper and Wilfred [Harper], Bob Lukin, Hassell, and Geoff Lukin, and some others I knew. They were cheery and confident, and soon passed on. A few minutes later a terrific burst of fire told us our first line had gone. There was a short lull of scattered fire then another burst more furious than the first signalled the second line had moved. Blocks ahead made our progress slow, and we found the bottom of the trench fairly littered with wounded men trying to get back for aid. With difficulty we passed them only to be blocked again, and word came back that some of the 8th LH were in the

trench in front. A third burst of fire, followed soon by a fourth and fifth, told us our chaps were still moving. Still we were blocked. A few men trickled past belonging to the 8th LH. A few minutes later came to order 'about turn', and we filed out again.[10]

Shortly after the third line had gone out into the fire storm, a scribbled message came back from Major Todd. It said that his line was pinned down unable to move forward, and asked for further orders. Brazier recalled the moment:

> The message was on a bit of pink paper. I took it back to Antill who refused to listen to me, and ordered me to push on again. I made him write it on the paper. On getting back to the trench again – only 15 or 20 yards – there was a similar message from Major Scott, on the right flank, asking for instructions. I would not go to Antill again as he had never left his trench, and looked for the Brigadier. After explaining the position and telling him it was murder to push on he said: 'try Bully Beef Sap'!![11]

This time Brazier had decided to ignore Antill's demands, and had to spend some time looking to find Hughes. While he was doing this, others were looking for him. In another account of his confrontation, Brazier says that he told Hughes that 'the whole thing was nothing but a "bloody murder"'.[12]

The next minutes are heavily clouded by the fog of war. Scott was waiting to learn what the absent Brazier had to say before committing his line to the attack. Because of the noise from the firing he told his troop leaders to order the next movement forward with a wave. His men waited tensely for the signal.

Suddenly, and without any signal having been given by Scott, the troops on the right rose out of their trenches and saps and rushed forward in a charge. 'By God, I believe the right has gone!' he cried in dismay.[13]

One of those in the fourth line, Sergeant William Sanderson, was later able to confirm that a signal had been passed along. Where it had started nobody could tell. Sanderson had seen Captain Rowan wave, then get up, be struck, and immediately fall back dead. Sanderson passed on the signal then climbed out and ran for the enemy's trench as hard as he could.

In his own account Sanderson said that Troopers Weston, Biggs and Hill charged alongside him. Weston and Biggs dropped, then he saw Hill spin around and fall, shot through the stomach. Glancing back over his shoulder he saw the only remaining men all falling together. In that moment, he tripped over a rhododendron bush and lay where he fell, hardly daring to move.[14]

Major Scott was able to stop the last line's attack before all the men left the trench and were lost. It is difficult to establish who made up the two lines of the 10th Light Horse. The few remaining records, including the official historian's account, do not agree. What is clear is that the men who took part in the assault met the same fate as their comrades in the 8th Regiment.

Lieutenant Kidd wrote:

> When the order 'Advance Third Line' came, with the exception of 1 troop, we leapt the parapet and the four troops on the right were practically annihilated before they could advance 5 yards. I went over with my troop, it was necessary to move to the right front in order to gain the neck. The pace was slow owing to the heaped up dead, rubble, bush, and wire. A slight depression in the ground afforded us a little protection, advantage of which had been seized by men of the 8th regiment who had escaped the holocaust. Just as we were forcing our way over the slight protecting rise, the order to 'Halt and Dig In' passed down the line.[15]

Another officer, Hugo Throssell, had arrived on Anzac just in time to take part in the attack. 'I am to lead you in a charge and it is the first time I have ever done such a thing,' he said. 'If any man doubts me, let him step forward now, and he may go with someone more experienced.' All of them followed him out into the fire. When it was seen that the task was absolutely impossible, he hastily ordered his men to throw themselves on to the ground. Most managed to take some cover in a small hollow, where the lieutenant shouted cheerily: 'A bob in and the winner shouts.'[16]

The 10th Light Horse's lines had proceeded more carefully than the two that had gone before them. Being pledged to go, the men climbed out of their trench but few felt any obligation to throw their lives away needlessly and most quickly sought any available cover. In one line a youth, Trooper Charles Williams, was placed between his sergeant and the squadron sergeant major. These older men were aware of the soldier's age and told him to get down as soon as he was out of the trench. Even before he could do this he was pulled to the ground.[17] In this way he became one of the survivors.

At least two pairs of brothers, including the Harper boys, were killed in the 10th Light Horse. Ross and Lindsay Chipper were farmers from Claremont who died in A Squadron's charge. Both were buried, just a few metres apart, in the Ari Burnu cemetery. Edmund MacGregor was one of the troopers detailed to carry ammunition but was not called forward. He waited anxiously in the trenches, knowing that his brother, Fred, had gone over the top. He later found him safe. Sergeant Duncan Bain was one of those killed when the right of the fourth line broke away. His brother was on the left and did not leave the trench. The sergeant was brought in dying, but his brother could not reach him in time. He attended his burial in the same cemetery in which the Chippers and many more of the bodies recovered that day were laid.

There were pairs of brothers among the 8th Light Horse too. The Cole boys, Dyson and Lionel, were just 19 and 21 years old. They had left the farm at Cobrico and enlisted together the previous September. Both had been mortally wounded and were carried down to the beach for evacuation. Lionel died before sundown while Dyson lingered until the following day. They were buried at sea. Albert and Alexander Evans had been Gippsland farmers; their bodies were never recovered. Lieutenant Keith Borthwick lay out dead on the battlefield but his brother was one of the survivors.

Norman Bethune lost his brother Douglas in the first wave. His only wish now was to recover his body. He explained to their sisters:

> We were unable to get any of our dead in except just a few who were a few yards out, and therefore we had very faint hope at first that some might have escaped, and would manage to get in at night time … At first we hoped to be able to go out that night and bring in any we could, and I of course volunteered to be one of a party. The Turks however all that night kept up a continuous rain of fire on the ground … and we weren't allowed to go out. I can hardly realise that we have lost him. I can't write about things like this …[18]

After part of the brigade's fourth line left, and the fire was beginning to die away, Major Love climbed out again to see what had happened. He managed to get to Todd, and near to McLaurin. They agreed that it was impossible to move forward, so Love and Todd inched their way back and, unknown to Brazier, set out to find Hughes. Getting back into the trench at some stage, Love fell heavily on his knee, damaging it badly and causing it to swell to the size of a football.

When the two officers reached the brigadier, they saw that he was clearly rattled. They insisted that no more progress could be made and that the battle was over. Hughes may have chosen to ignore Love, but he had to listen to Todd. He told them to gather the surviving men, and go around by Bully Beef Sap to support the Royal Welch Fusiliers. The brigadier had already sent two companies of the Cheshire Regiment into Monash Valley to assist the fusiliers, who had discovered that their task was as impossible as that of the light horsemen.

Two companies of the British 8th Royal Welch Fusiliers had arrived on Anzac only a few days before and were under Lieutenant Colonel Hay, a regular army officer who would survive this day only to be killed 18 months later. The leading company, led by Captain Walter Lloyd, an officer recently brought out of retirement, tried to advance while another company was pinned down by Turkish machine-guns. Lloyd led his men up impossible ground from the direction of Monash Gully; they could only advance in single file, ten men at a time. They had barely begun when they came under terrible fire, including bombs which were rolled down on them. Lloyd was among those killed. Attacking up the steep slope of the valley into deadly fire was suicidal. Hay ordered a halt and sent a message to Hughes.

It is hard to imagine what Hughes had in mind for the light horsemen. Two of his regiments had been cut to pieces and most of the senior officers, troop leaders and NCOs were dead, wounded or dazed. It was quite impossible to reorganise the exhausted survivors into a fresh assault elsewhere. Before anything could be done, the word came back that the British attack had failed. The brigadier's insistence on trying to have his light horsemen assist the attack across Monash Valley shows his failure to grasp the situation.

Hughes had not taken proper command. When he left his headquarters to find an observation spot, he unwittingly split the control of the brigade. Antill had no hesitation in giving orders to keep the attack going, as he believed he was correctly interpreting the commanders' instructions. After the third line had left, Hughes realised that another effort could not succeed, so he called off the attack. However, as orders were emanating from two points, there was inevitable confusion.

The actions of other officers had also compounded the problems. While Brazier was chasing around trying to have the attacks stopped, Reynell was encouraging Antill to continue. He later wrote:

> I felt so strongly that it could get forward that I reported to the Brigade Major that if he gave me authority to do so I would guarantee to get the trenches with the men of the 8th and 10th that were there. However an order was sent to them to rush the trenches but the officers on the spot considered it impossible and they were withdrawn.[19]

The order to fall back was sent out to the survivors in no-man's-land. Those who could carefully made their way in, although several were killed in the effort. Others waited all day until darkness provided some cover. Artillery fire was now falling on the Turks' lines and the diversion gave some the chance to get back to safety.

Sanderson, from the fourth wave, had lain in an advanced position for half an hour. Looking back, he saw Captain Phil Fry kneeling up outside the secret sap, then Todd appeared beside him and shouted something that sounded like 'retire the 4th line first'.[20]

Sanderson was among those who began to crawl back. When he finally got close in, he found an officer of the 8th Light Horse – it was probably young Anderson – with a frightful wound. This man had been carrying some bombs in a haversack. These had been hit by a round, causing them to explode, blowing his whole hip away. He was screaming in agony. When some men tried to get him in, he begged them to leave him alone: 'I can't bloody well stand it,' he cried. They did get him back in, but he died on the floor of the sap.

Sanderson saw that the front line was surrounded by a ring of bodies. Most seemed to be from the 8th Light Horse. Once he was safely back he noted that the trenches too were full of the dead, the suffering and the maimed.[21] Among those of his regiment who had been mortally hit, he could recognise Turnbull, Rowan, Weston and Hill.

Captain Andrew Rowan had been killed instantly by bullets through the head and chest as he climbed out of his trench. Tall and powerfully built, this popular officer, who was four weeks from his 40th birthday, already wore a medal ribbon from his time as a young officer in the South African War. He had retained a commission in the militia before going on to the reserve in 1910, and shortly afterwards taking up farming in Western Australia. When Brazier had accepted Rowan for a commission in the AIF, he had noted that he seemed 'a manly, decent gentlemen [who] should do well'.[22]

Rowan had been wounded at Quinn's Post earlier but had soldiered on, and in July had been made a captain. News of his death cut his sister Violet deeply. Her grief became anger and she reacted, wanting proof of her brother's death, and seeking to have his body returned to the family. Most of all, although not knowing the facts, she blamed Brazier for his loss: 'I was in WA when my brother's regiment was being trained under the biggest fool at this game ever known. I mean the commanding officer … I am quite sure he alone is responsible for any mistakes that may have been made.'[23]

Alexander Turnbull gasped his last breath in the dirt on the floor of the sap. The second lieutenant had held a commission for just a matter of days and was one of two Rhodes scholars at this battle. He was from a well-known landed family in the Esperance district, and had been practising law in Perth when he joined the light horse. Turnbull had gained some previous military experience while at Oxford, where he served for three years in King Edward's Horse, in a squadron made up of expatriate Australians. When the cables were received telling of the deaths of Turnbull and the Harper brothers, the *West Australian* newspaper was moved to comment that 'these three young men, each of them a native of the state, were so widely known and highly esteemed that the news of their tragic deaths at an age and time when life seemed so possessed of such great possibilities for them will be a sad reading for many.'[24]

If anyone could be braver than those who charged into the Turks' fire, it has to be those who, on their own initiative, gave up their safety to go out and rescue the wounded. Trumpeter Les Lawry, who was just 19 and had to get his parents' permission when he joined up, brought in several men, including the dying Anderson. His work was recognised by his being mentioned in despatches.[25]

Another was Trooper Martin O'Donoghue, who managed to bring in a comrade, and wrote about the man he rescued:

He was hit on the back with a bomb and died afterwards. He was a fine fellow. I seemed terribly lucky when I was carrying him in. They were all crying out, 'Leave him there, you will get hit yourself', but the bullets seemed just to miss me. It was not for bravery that I did it. I could not stand seeing him there, moaning in agony.[26]

The following month O'Donoghue was himself hit by a bomb; he died an agonising death three months later from blood poisoning.

Lance Corporal Billy Hampshire became a hero among the Western Australians that morning. Already, some weeks earlier, he had been commended for his 'coolness and courage' when his trench was blown in by Turkish shellfire. He went out with his squadron at The Nek and, after getting back to safety, returned to rescue his troop leader, Lieutenant Leslie Craig, whose foot had been shot away. He then went out again and brought in two more badly wounded men. Finally, Sergeant MacBean had to physically restrain him and order him to cease risking his own life.[27]

Lieutenant Craig survived and after a long hospitalisation was invalided home. Following the war he became a member of parliament and was well-known in returned soldier circles in the west. Hampshire was made a sergeant, but soon afterwards was seriously wounded; in January 1916 he was returned to Australia and discharged from the AIF six months later.

Major McLaurin, his face covered in blood, had stayed out in front after having helped recover Anderson. When the word to retire was received, he coolly gave orders to see that the remnants of his regiment got back safely. He was the last man to get in from the left section of the line.[28]

A witness to the whole sad affair was Sergeant Clifford Ashburner, a former professional boxer and South African War veteran who commanded a machine-gun at Turks' Point. In the hours leading up to the attack he had poured thousands of rounds into the Turkish lines as part of the preparation. During the charge he could see the Turks standing breast-high above their trenches as they shot the light horsemen down:

The first and 2nd lines went out running – charging. The 3rd line bent, with rifles on guard, walking. When they got as far as the knoll they turned, and those who could get back to the trenches did so. Then a long time before the last lot.

Without orders, Ashburner brought his gun back into action, but was soon ordered to stop by Reynell, who believed that the Australians had got into the enemy lines. The sergeant received a message: 'Aren't you firing on our own men?' When the firing subsided, he could see the dead and wounded lying out in no-man's-land. 'Scaling ladders had been dropped by the first party. Could see men trying to drink out of bottle[s], and raising arms, but within 3 or 4 hours they seemed to be dead.'[29]

The battle for The Nek was over. Brazier, and some others, stood looking in disbelief at the front trench where stunned, wounded and dying men were almost the only occupants. He took his periscope and watched no-man's-land, now littered with the crumpled and bloodied khaki heaps of many of his men. For half an hour he looked over the sorry sight, fearing that at any moment the Turks would surge forward in a counter-attack. If they had come they could easily have overrun the Australians' positions. Fortunately, with heavy fighting elsewhere, they had to let this opportunity pass.

Lieutenant Robinson of the 8th Light Horse later recalled: 'I tried to discuss the affair with some survivors of my regiment. Some seemed half stunned and dazed. One was sobbing like a lost child three years of age and another laughed hysterically whenever I spoke to him.'[30] Tom Austin made a similar observation: 'Many of the men on the cliff face were so shaken that they were almost helpless and the evacuations during the ensuing days from shock were heart-breaking.'[31]

Trooper MacGregor remembered: 'We were shattered, absolutely shattered. It was the hardest [time] of the whole war. Later looking out on the dead was horrible. We were in a sort of coma – dopey. We never discussed it later. We couldn't.'[32]

Corporal McGrath found some of the survivors of his squadron. He saw 'most of these were in such a state of shock that it was impossible to get coherency'.[33] McConnan reported that he felt 'fed up'.[34] Sergeant Pinnock admitted that when the fighting was over he 'cried like a child'.[35] One confused and angry soldier threatened Major Love with a bayonet in the mistaken belief that the officer had not left the trenches.[36] Even tough old Tom Todd, who had returned unwounded after leading the third line, later collapsed from the stress and was eventually evacuated to England to recover.[37]

About 200 men had gone over the top not to return. The parents of Lieutenant Higgins eventually heard that he was safe. He wrote to them describing the battle and the friends he had lost:

Most of them are still reported missing as it is impossible in cases to find someone who either saw them killed or lying dead afterwards. We were only able to get in a few bodies, and most of those who are still out will probably be unrecognisable by this time, as there has been a good deal of bombing going on.[38]

When the figures were finally assembled it was established that the 8th Light Horse had 234 casualties, killed and wounded, from 300 men, while the 10th had 138.[39]

Although he overestimated the number of Turkish machine-guns, Walter McConnan summed up the experience with his impressions:

Instead of a soft snap, as many of us thought, we had to climb out into the hottest fire you could imagine. There must have been 20 machine-guns and thousands of rifles on us. My regiment went to the peninsula full strength [over 500 men] and I suppose our reinforcements have numbered 250, yet our strength last Sunday [a fortnight after the attack] was about 60.[40]

CHAPTER 12

The Aftermath
of Battle

The day of tragedy passed slowly on Russell's Top. A stream of shocked and wounded survivors made their way to the aid posts and the dressing stations, while the recovered bodies of the dead were carried down to the cemeteries where they were laid in rows for burial. In front of The Nek the slain lay thick in crumpled heaps while the immobile, bloody from their wounds, remained where they fell, dying out of reach of any help. The suffering was pitiful but, as the day grew hotter, one by one their agonies ceased as death overtook them. Most of the survivors of the 8th Light Horse were gathered just behind Walker's Ridge; they were in no state for any further action. The remnants of the rest of the brigade, mostly the 9th Regiment and some of the 10th, and the British troops, stood waiting expectantly for a counter-attack which mercifully never came.

The next few days saw more heavy fighting at various points at Anzac, but the grand plan to regain the offensive had failed. The British corps had got ashore at Suvla but no important advantage was ever derived from this. Lone Pine had been captured and, in succeeding days, it was defiantly held against wild counter-attacks. But Lone Pine had only been intended as a diversion to assist the main efforts elsewhere. The New Zealanders did get onto Chunuk Bair, but only to see it lost again, turning that short victory into another sorry disaster.

The 3rd Light Horse Brigade had suffered grievously. The 8th Regiment was no longer an effective fighting force and it would be some time before it could be built up and used again. The shortage of officers throughout the brigade was so acute that among the promotions which soon followed there were a number of corporals and lance corporals who received commissions.

It was difficult for the light horsemen to accept the scale of their losses for no gain at all. Arthur Olden, who had been a lieutenant with the 10th Light Horse on Gallipoli, later wrote: 'Bitter as was the loss of their comrades, it was nothing compared with the bitterness of the knowledge that their lives were offered up in vain.'[1]

For a few days men clung on to some misguided hopes that the efforts had been worthwhile, but these soon evaporated and disillusion set in. A week after the battle an officer in the 10th Regiment wrote in his diary: 'We now realise we have failed. Before the attack the Regiment was buoyant, excited and hopeful. Now its aspirations are shattered like an electric globe. Our hopes are frozen tears.'[2]

Reynell had been optimistic before the battle, but his diary records a more sombre attitude in the days afterwards. He acknowledges the impossibility of the task and as he began to accept the failure of the offensive a sense of despondency crept over him, as the following extracts show:

After 6 weeks of influenza and dysentery I wasn't very fit when the attack started and trusted to the excitement to keep me going. I am feeling very limp with headache, neuralgia, sore throat, cold in the head and chesty and pant like a grampus with the least exertion. Our offensive has come to a stop everywhere and there is no sign of revival. Into the bargain we are all ill to breaking point …

The attack … showed that the confined space across which any attack must be made is so swept by converging fire from rifle and machine-gun fire that no living thing can cross it. Each line as they reached a certain zone were just mowed down instantaneously and some men's legs were completely severed by machine-gun fire. Not one got back except those who either didn't get as far as this zone or who were wounded and dropped into dead ground and returned on their [bellies] in dead ground or came back after dark. I am ill, the officers – that there are left, are ill, the whole Regiment is ill, the army corps is ill and the news is ill.

Well I have seen more war the last week than one might ordinarily in years of war. [The Australians] are a d – d sight better tribe than I ever thought. Their dash and pluck I hoped was there. Their initiative and resource I knew was there. But their dogged determination, patience and cheerful fortitude I never believed in – but it's there too.[3]

The brigade remained on Russell's Top for just a short while longer, ready to repulse any Turkish attack. Some men were detached to try to recover bodies, while others were sent to join burial parties. Disinfectant – usually nothing more than lime, or an unlikely mixture described as petrol mixed with water – was distributed in the trenches because of the decaying bodies.[4] Grappling irons were thrown out, and one of the forward saps was extended so that some of the dead could be reached. Major Redford's body was among those dragged in.

It was ten days before Sergeant Cameron, who had been in charge of some of the sharpshooters in the 9th Light Horse providing covering fire, was able to find the time to bring his diary up to date.

We had some severe fighting and it turns out that we have gained little in territory or position, yet sacrificed thousands of lives. The Turkish Machine-Guns just poured out lead and our fellows went down like the corn before a scythe. [Resumes next day.] Four hundred and ninety casualties in less than a quarter of an hour.[5] Yes, it was heroic, it was marvellous, the way those men rose, yet it was murder. We are still holding Russell's Top, and the strain is telling terribly on all ranks. Whenever one looks in the direction of the Turkish trenches one sees the bodies of our own chaps in almost the same places as were the bodies of the Turks after 30th June. Nothing can be done to get them buried or brought in except those which are very close to our own trench. The smell is dreadful. Nothing can compare with decomposed human flesh for horror. The intervening space is continually lit by flares and bombs and several bodies have been burnt thus. It seems cruel, but from the health point it is better, whoever does the burning.[6]

Captain Callary of the 9th Light Horse had been observing alongside Reynell during the attack and had seen the other regiments' heavy losses. He wrote home: 'No doubt you got a shock when you noticed our [brigade's] casualties. Never shall I forget the morning when we lined up in the rear of them. We have had some sad losses but Turkey is paying for it.'[7]

In the 8th Light Horse, 13 officers had been killed, and of the remaining six who took part, only Deeble and Higgins remained unmarked.[8] Hore, Robinson and Crawford were evacuated with their wounds, while McLaurin, who had returned to duty on the 13th, could only hold on for a fortnight before he had to go away. Deeble was evacuated to hospital within a week, and Higgins had to be sent off for a rest. In the 10th Regiment, seven officers were dead and, among the seriously wounded, Robinson and Craig were returned to Australia. Soon afterwards Major Love's badly injured leg required that he be sent to Australia for an extended period. Antill was glad to be rid of him. He did not return to the regiment until after the campaign was over and then he was mostly engaged in staff and training work.[9]

An officer of the 10th Light horse wrote:

The men carry on and do their duty, but each man seems to be brooding over the possibilities of 'what might have been'. He does not speak for fear of starting the same train of thought in his mate. He has not appreciated the fact that his mate is thinking exactly the same unuttered thoughts.[10]

The enemy's view of the action at The Nek first became known after a couple of Turks became prisoners of war and told their stories. The Nek and Baby 700 were occupied by parts of the 19th Division. This was an 'Ottoman' division as it consisted of both Turkish (18th, 27th, and 57th) and Arab (72nd and 77th) regiments; the latter were less highly regarded as fighting units. In command of the division was Mustafa Kemal Atatürk, who was destined to become Turkey's greatest military leader and statesman of the twentieth century.

Battalions of infantry from the 18th and 27th Regiments were opposing the light horsemen. These were good regiments raised over a wide region and already contained a core of regular soldiers who were veterans of the Balkan Wars, and many who had been fighting at Anzac since April. Some of the officers had been trained by the Germans. Very shortly after moving into the line at The Nek, the 18th Regiment had been ordered to make its ill-fated attack of 29 June. Their losses had been severe but they were still not given any relief. Even before this the regiment had lost its popular commanding officer, whose fearlessness had resulted in his becoming an early casualty of Australian snipers.

Most of the Turkish private soldiers were from villages, and many could neither read nor write. But they were tough and well-armed with modern rifles, machine-guns and hand bombs. Fortunately for the Australians they did not have a lot of artillery. Their uniforms were rough and usually ragged, a lot of their equipment was handmade, and they wore an assortment of footwear with just a few having stout boots. Sergeant Norman Worrall, in the 8th Light Horse, had noted that 'they seem to wear their private clothes in addition to their uniforms ... were loaded up with about 350 rounds of ammunition, and had their haversacks full of provisions [and] have very good rifles'.[11]

The Australians had been quick to recognise their opponents' fighting abilities – although what else could they do when their own bravery and determination were constantly being matched? Most of the Turks were devout Muslims and they were defending their homeland.

For the Turks, like the Australians, life in the trenches was hard. They suffered most of the same deprivations, there was no inoculation against disease, and their rations were poor; bread and soup were their staples. Conditions became more dangerous as the British guns commenced their shelling in the days leading up to the big offensive. During the night of 6 August the firing seemed constant, a shell bursting every five or ten minutes. There were many casualties and these continued to mount as dawn drew closer.

The Turks knew from the preparatory fire that an assault on The Nek could be expected. A captured soldier, a former schoolteacher, told Charles Bean that he had noticed a pause between the shelling and the appearance of the first wave of light horsemen. He and his comrades were two deep in their front trench with the forward rank behind the parapet and the rear one standing behind them. Each man had his bayonet fixed, but these were not needed as their rifle fire and machine-guns swept the Australian attacks away. Within an hour they had settled their score with the invaders. After the battle the regiment received a special order from their commander complimenting the men on their performance; in addition several awards were given and promotions made.[12]

In late August troops of the 2nd Australian Division began arriving at Anzac. One of the infantry battalions, the 20th, was sent up to Russell's Top where it took over from the light horse brigade. This single battalion could provide a similar number of men in the line to that of a brigade of light horse. The survivors of The Nek fighting were glad to be at last able to leave this place, where so many of their comrades had been slain. The fresh arrivals received quite a shock. The small space between their own trenches and the enemy's had been a slaughterhouse. Victor Portman, who had joined the 20th Battalion after having already taken part in the capture of German New Guinea, recalled:

> The bodies of more than 200 light horsemen still lay on the parapet and in the scrub within a few hundred yards of our post. There was a frightful reek of death, and huge swarms of flies seethed over the place, living on the dead and poisoning the living. The trench walls in places were reinforced with dead men and everywhere on the surface of the ground were limbs and bodies, adrift in the debris of smashed rifles, bloody equipment and the flotsam and jetsam of the mad battles fought in the scrub and tangle of those harsh, forbidding slopes in early August.[13]

The infantrymen set about clearing up the mess of battles, and in the following weeks lengthened and developed the front line. Further sapping extended their reach into no-man's-land, and more bodies could be recovered. The memory of these corpses haunted Portman. Referring to the dead, he wrote:

> All of this unhappy band wore pith helmets and shorts. The positions of several of them had given us some very vivid memories. About five yards from the parapet of the post I first had on The Nek, one of them faced us on his hands and knees. He had evidently been wounded and had started to crawl back to the trench when a second bullet killed him. A bush on one side had held him in that position, and the sentry on this post had to look straight into his face while observing. In the night time the only thing one could see was the faint smudge of the man's figure, and his face always seemed to be asking a question. Sentries could not stand that for very long, so we had to remove him. Another dead man was found lying under a bush with his prayer book in his hand, and half of it ripped clean away as though cut by a knife.

It was inevitable that many survivors within the light horse brigade should try to place the responsibility for the calamity on somebody. In the few weeks after the battle there was a heavy undercurrent of anger and disillusionment. The tendency among the men in the ranks to blame the faceless officers 'high up' deflected some of the attention from the local commanders. Within the brigade The Nek became known as 'Godley's abattoir'.[14]

Brazier was furious. He blamed Hughes and Antill for the disaster that had befallen his regiment, and he made his anger and resentment known. His frustrations had turned to blind contempt. Hughes had found him difficult to work with earlier, but now he was impossible. Deciding that he would have to tell Godley of Brazier's behaviour and recommend that he be sent back home, Hughes wrote:

> His manner lately has been anything but respectful and he has chosen to adopt an attitude which I cannot but regard as objurgate, litigious and sullen. He resents being corrected and acts in such a way as to make it utterly distasteful and almost impossible to have anything to do with him. His demeanour is such that the present situation cannot continue and I therefore reluctantly, after the most careful consideration, feel it my duty to report him as quite unsuitable for the office of command on active service and accordingly recommend that he be struck off the strength of the Brigade and returned to Australia.[15]

Brazier tried to defend himself, but after speaking to Godley he saw that 'things looked quite against me'.[16] Eventually, he was told that he should resign to avoid being sacked. However, at the height of the dispute, and before his resignation was effective, he received a nasty wound to the left eye from a shrapnel ball when the camp of the 10th Light Horse was shelled.

Brazier was evacuated. His wound would leave him blind in one eye and force his return home. He declared bitterly that it was 'goodbye to Antill and two wars'. He briefly resumed an association with the militia in Western Australia, and for six months in 1917 was attached to the Sea Transport Service looking after the movement of troops, but took no further fighting part in the war. He remained bitter about his treatment, and about the conduct of the Gallipoli campaign, for the rest of his life.[17]

Despite the horror of their experiences at The Nek, the regiments were not spared from further heavy fighting during the rest of August. Immediately after it was relieved on Russell's Top, the brigade was again in action at Hill 60, where an attempt was made to improve the link between the Anzac and Suvla positions.

At Hill 60 the 9th and 10th Light Horse Regiments were thrown into another attempt to capture the Turks' trenches. Again losses were high, and many of the 9th Regiment, who had been spared their part in The Nek disaster, died here. Among the officers, both Reynell, who had assumed command, and Callary were killed not far from each other, while Cameron, who had just recently been commissioned, was mortally hit as the regiment was being relieved.

Of the Western Australians, Phil Fry and Colin MacBean, who had been at The Nek, were among the officers now dead. Major Scott and Lieutenants Kidd and Throssell were again lucky and survived to be commended for their good work. Hugo Throssell was subsequently awarded the Victoria Cross, the only light horseman to receive the highest award for gallantry.

The fighting in August 1915 remained the brigade's worst experience during the entire war. All three regiments suffered severely at The Nek, or at Hill 60. The effects were deeply felt and even Antill became despondent. During the fighting at Hill 60, he wrote:

> No particulars yet of the 9th and 10th casualties last 2 days but hear they are heavy and serious – At this rate we shall have absolutely no neucleus [sic] to rebuild upon: but nobody seems to care – merely fill the gap, get blown out, and done with – The feeling on this point is particularly strong and our troops are being butchered to try to make good for the recent drafts of men from Eng[land].[18]

Within a fortnight family and friends in Australia began to get word of the disaster which had befallen the brigade. At first it was the private and official telegrams advising a next of kin of a death. Then newspaper stories began to appear. Often wives or parents learnt of their loss from their local church minister or priest, who would have received advice from the Department of Defence asking that they break the sad news and provide comfort. One of those who took on this burden throughout the war was Canon Hughes, brother of the brigadier. He delivered the tragic messages around inner Melbourne and sometimes to the suburbs. Friends saw how the strain affected him; he was one of many.

The Victorian town of Hamilton lost at least three men at The Nek. On

19 August Archdeacon Harris was asked to advise Ted Henty's young wife that he had died on the 7th. There were no other details. Shortly afterwards the local newspaper, in publishing the death notice, had also to report that one of its own former employees, Trooper William Hind, had died in the same attack.[19]

In the following days more news came in. In Perth a private cable, which was passed to a local newspaper, advised that the Harper brothers and Lieutenant Turnbull had been killed. In the absence of any formal reports, rumours of a disaster involving the state's light horse regiment spread. The premier was approached for information, so on 26 August he sent a telegram to the Department of Defence seeking confirmation or a denial. The minister could only advise that heavy casualties had been reported and that more details were awaited.[20]

By late September the correspondents' cables had arrived, and the full extent of the disaster became apparent as the casualty lists were released. Charles Bean submitted a vivid account of the fighting at The Nek and edited versions were taken by some of the newspapers.[21]

Very few of Bean's stories from Gallipoli were censored. However, in this instance the scissors and blue pencil removed parts of the typescript, and the Commonwealth censor made an amendment before this official version was released. It is notable that although Bean had twice written that the yellow-and-red marker flag had flown for just two minutes after the 8th Light Horse attacked, the censor evidently felt more comfortable in altering this to 10 minutes. If there had been a flag seen for a longer time, this would better explain why the attack was allowed to continue. Bean's account may have been slightly softened in this way, but it did remain substantially unchanged.

The losses from the battle were widely felt. Some larger towns found that they lost several of their young men in the August offensive, and often a few of these had died at The Nek. Some homes lost more than one son, and there were instances of cousins dying together. Other smaller communities – Marong in central Victoria was one – were to mourn the loss of their first local boy. There would be others to follow.

The congregation of the Presbyterian church at Armadale, in Melbourne, had been praying for the safety of Keith Borthwick. The death of the lieutenant removed the first soldier from their church community. A local youngster, Brian Lewis, remembered the news being received and, in describing it, gave a brief glimpse into his own household. Three of his mother's relatives had been killed and a cousin's fiancé, one of the Cole brothers, was among them. The cousin was to lose her fiancé, father and brother in the war. Lewis recalled that 'mother asked her to stay with us to cheer her up, but she remained pretty miserable'.[22]

Some of the light horsemen had been schoolmates. When the news was received that a couple of its former students had died, the flag at Hamilton College was flown at half mast. Melbourne Grammar School had half a dozen old boys killed in this small action, and the Scotch College recorded four deaths.

Many parents or wives would eventually receive letters from their dead soldiers' mates expressing sympathy and giving the details of the battle so anxiously sought by the families. Until his own death, Lieutenant Colonel White found writing these letters very painful. The people at home may have been told of their sons' 'glorious deaths', but back on Gallipoli their bodies lay mutilated and rotting, stinking and feeding the flies until after December, when the hills became quiet again and the wild animals came down to scatter the bones.

The Irish parents of Trooper Henry McNeill of the 10th Regiment received a typical letter describing their boy's part in the charge. It went on:

> When we had to retire to the trenches that we started from, I looked for your son and to my sorrow could see him lying a few yards out. I watched him for a few minutes and could not see him move. That night we got him and several more in and carried them down to our medical station. We could not bury them that night, as we could not be spared from the firing line for long, but the next night we carried your son down and gave him a decent burial, our Army Chaplain reading the burial service and saying a short prayer. We mounded his grave up with stones and put a small wooden cross at the head of it with his name and regiment on it.[23]

David Griffith's squadron sergeant-major wrote to his parents in Wales:

> Your son was in my squadron and I was near him when he was killed. I thought a lot of him, and am proud to say he was a pal of mine. We were in such a very bad place; our regiment made a grand name for themselves. You can always feel proud he belonged to the 8th L.H.

We were set a very bad task that morning but console yourself he died nobly doing his bit like the fearless boy he was.[24]

Hundreds of households were thrown into mourning by the tragic charge of the light horse on that fateful day, and it was women, and sometimes children, who carried the major part of this burden. Their sorrowful stories remain one of the least recorded aspects of the war experience. Many years afterwards Trooper Michael Larkin's mother was asked to complete a form confirming his personal details for the nation's roll of honour. She provided the simple facts as requested, but was compelled by her pride and sorrow to add that he was 'one of the best and bravest men that left these shores'.[25] A mother's simple notation, to be stumbled upon by future researchers, carried more impact than the name and initials borne on any bronze roll of honour.

Other equally poignant expressions are to be seen as epitaphs on the headstones of the few men whose graves on Gallipoli can be identified in the cemetery at Ari Burnu. Among these, Sergeant Rawlings' mother had written in stone: 'My only darling son'. Trooper Northey's family wrote: 'Our loved son and bro. One of the best'. Trooper Cumming's people had the words 'Rest dear son rest. Sadly missed' inscribed on his headstone.

Mervyn Higgins survived the charge, but his death the following year was further evidence of the tragedy of that war. This officer continued to serve with the 8th regiment until a sniper got him in the forehead, just above the left eye, at Magdhaba on 23 December. He had survived the gale of bullets at The Nek to be killed by a single aimed shot. McLaurin was still serving with him and their friendship had been welded by their common experiences on Gallipoli. McLaurin stayed with the body of his dead colleague until an ambulance wagon came up in the evening to take him away. It was dark so they waited until next day, Christmas Eve, to prepare his grave.

Young Higgins's death was a brutal blow to his parents. 'My grief has condemned me to hard labour for the rest of my life,' declared his father.[26] He and his wife were united in their shared sorrow until they died. After the war they journeyed to Egypt to visit their son's grave, and then went to Magdhaba to see where he had died seven years earlier. A Celtic cross was erected as a memorial in the Dromana cemetery, the Mervyn Higgins Bursary Fund was endowed to help students at Ormond College, and a shield was presented for the annual inter-college boat race. This family was able to express its sorrow publicly, but their loss was an experience too common throughout the war years.

The consequences of the losses at The Nek were felt within the AIF and far beyond. In many ways the disaster typified the Gallipoli campaign and, in particular, the failure of the August offensive. The story of the attack became quickly known among the men of Anzac. The awareness that lives could be lost for no gain, and that commanders could make large-scale and fatal blunders, had an effect on morale. After the Australian journalist Keith Murdoch visited Anzac in September 1915, he reported to the Prime Minister that the Australians 'loathe and detest' the English staff officers.[27] The repercussions from the failed offensive extended throughout the entire force and ultimately affected its character. There was little likelihood that by 1918 Australian officers or men would have accepted tasks such as they had attempted on 7 August 1915.

The official historian had seen just how great the impact of the disaster had been, and later wrote: 'With the exception of the attempt of the 4th Infantry Brigade ... the following day, no other experience in 1915 was so powerful to create that disillusionment which superseded the first fine fervour of Australian soldiers.'[28]

CHAPTER 13

Reflection

The attack at the Nek had been a disaster on two major counts. First, it had totally failed to achieve its military objective, and second, the commanders had not acted to minimise the casualties. In trying to apportion responsibility, both these aspects have to be considered.

The attack was just a part of the larger scheme, which had been devised to revitalise the campaign. The general concept of a breakout from Anzac, proposed by Birdwood and Skeen, had been sound enough. In broad terms, the plan seemed logical and reasonable. As planning progressed, however, and the details were considered, the immensity of the task must have become apparent. Even the over-confident Skeen must have had reservations when he began to consider the enemy's strengths, the nature and extent of his defences, the terrible terrain over which the troops would have to operate and the poor physical condition of the men.

If there was to be a military victory on Gallipoli, bold and aggressive action was necessary, in which casualties would likely be heavy. Birdwood and Skeen understood this. After their experiences in India, they may have thought themselves well-qualified to consider operations in the wild hilly country facing Chunuk Bair and Hill 971. But here at Anzac things were a lot different. Skeen's successor, Brudenell White, later said that he thought the overall plan was a 'brilliant conception … but it totally disregarded the almost impossible nature of the country'.[1] They were not properly aware of the conditions and the problems they posed for men in declining health.

Their confidence was misplaced. At all the senior levels, the British leaders approached this campaign as some colonial military sideshow. There was an underlying presumption that British might must overcome the Turkish ragtag army. And even after they discovered the determination, skill and bravery of the enemy, they still failed to take these things into proper consideration. Often the Turkish successes were attributed to the leadership of German officers believed to be serving among them. However, this had far less to do with it than the British thought.

The August offensive at Anzac may have contained the germ of a good idea, but clearly the planning and conduct of the battles would have been handled differently if undertaken later in the war. For most of the participants – and this is true through all levels – these events took place early in their war.

The 'experienced' officers were usually those who had served in South Africa, or possibly India. The senior commanders, like Birdwood and some of his staff, could claim both. Many of these officers had assumed that they held a natural and military superiority over the Boers and now, 15 years later, they made a similar assumption about the Turks – to their great cost. In both cases, they faced a formidable enemy well-supplied with arms by the Germans. Few lessons from the recent fighting on the Belgian and French fronts had any impact at Anzac.

Gallipoli was a curious mixture of old and modern warfare. Many of the most modern weapons and tactics were being employed, yet other equipment and practices were remarkably crude. The aeroplane and quick-firing artillery appeared alongside jam-tin bombs and massed bayonet charges. The lack of understanding of modern warfare, to which most of the officers had not yet been fully exposed, a failure to appreciate the impact of technology – especially the Turks' clever employment of machine-guns – and poor communications and staff work, all showed how little experience there was within the command structure. It was still believed that discipline and aggressive spirit were the essence of military success. There was no way to disguise the unpreparedness of these officers for the type of campaign they were now engaged upon. Many of them learnt quickly and went on to make important contributions but, among some others, deficiencies were soon exposed.

Addressing his whole corps before the great August battles, Birdwood wrote:

> I want you to remember that the fighting we shall probably have in this advance will be very much the same nature as it was on the day we landed. Then … we ignored all trenches – rushing at all we saw, chasing the Turks out of them, and keeping them well on the run. This we have to do again.[2]

Anyone reading this could be forgiven for thinking that the British had won the earlier battles, and should be able to do so again. Birdwood completely ignores the fact that the Turks had successfully held the advance and had forced the British on to the defensive.

The plan for 7 August proved to be overly ambitious and far too complex. It presumed too much, and so as each part became unstuck, the next failed as a consequence. The most important work was given to the New Zealanders and Monash's brigade. But their task would have been exhausting even under peacetime conditions.

Along the established front line, the debacle at German Officers' Trench was the first indication that things were beginning to come undone. The officers at The Nek, Quinn's Post and Pope's Hill knew that the objectives they had been given were unthinkable, unless there was some drastic change in the situation which had existed over the past few months. Even Birdwood and Skeen accepted this. Heavy supporting fire would provide the necessary change. This did not happen, and predictably the attacks were torn apart.

In their enthusiasm for a victory, Birdwood and Skeen had ignored their own better judgement, and so at The Nek they threw the light horsemen against the most solid ramparts on Anzac. They knew that they could not hope to concentrate enough force against such a narrow front with defences in such depth. Despite having previously written that 'an unaided attack' across The Nek and Baby 700 was 'almost hopeless', they sent the 3rd Light Horse Brigade in.[3]

The attack was ordered even after it was known that sufficient support was no longer available. The repulse of the infantry at German Officers' Trench meant that the Turks' machine-guns there could provide added deadly enfilading fire on Quinn's Post and The Nek once those attacks began. The artillery preparation had been well-maintained on The Nek, although it was poorly coordinated with the assault. But it had not yet been learnt just how intense shelling had to be for it to be fully effective against well-developed trench defences. This level of firepower was not available on Anzac; howitzers in particular were few. Finally, the converging attack from Chunuk Bair did not eventuate.

It had been Birdwood's decision to launch the assault. Knowing that the operations elsewhere were not proceeding well, he decided to accept losses at The Nek to assist the main attacks upon the heights, which he insisted must continue. At the same time, Skeen, who was at his side, showed that he did not fully understand the position: 'It is not the light horse I am anxious about. I think they will be all right. What I hope is that they will help the New Zealanders.'[4]

For The Nek Birdwood had devised a plan which never had much chance of success, and had placed the conduct of the attack in the hands of an officer in whom he had little confidence. By failing to replace Hughes, and by allowing Antill to exercise so much influence, Birdwood created a dual command, which would cause confusion at the height of the battle. Godley's lack of initiative just made matters worse. He took his orders from Birdwood without question and expected his own to be accepted in the same manner. He responded angrily if queried and refused to take advice which said the attack across The Nek must fail.

Godley certainly contributed heavily to the disaster. It was he who insisted that the attack had to be driven home at all costs. He may have been a good peacetime planner and organiser, but he failed to understand that determination and courage alone could not overcome intense machine-gun and rifle fire. Although he visited Russell's Top often enough, he too did little to understand what he was requiring that day of the men there and elsewhere. He made no attempt to stop the light horsemen's attacks although he was aware, at least to some extent, how badly they were progressing. In both his attitude and actions, there is nothing to suggest that, had Godley been in Antill's place, he would have acted any differently. In his report on the fighting at Quinn's Post, he only conceded that 'the Officer Commanding exercised what was *probably* a wise discretion in discontinuing the assault' (emphasis added).[5] Even Antill later condemned Godley's role, declaring with some bitterness: 'The responsibility of the attack and its result must rest with divisional headquarters. It was never encouraged or endorsed by brigade, and beyond a congratulatory mention in Anzac orders the disastrous affair was dropped and nothing more was heard of it.'[6]

It has sometimes been imagined that the attack had been partly successful because it held the Turks' attention and diverted them from reinforcing other parts of their line. This argument may have had some value if the British offensive had been successful, but it is negated by the fact that the losses had been so heavy as to expose Russell's Top to a possible enemy counter-attack. While a diversion may have been necessary, it could have been done in a less costly way. It was only because there was heavy fighting elsewhere that the Turks were forced to let this opportunity pass.

One can only speculate about the reason for the lag of several minutes between the end of the artillery shelling and the start of the attack. Clearly it was vital in enabling the Turks to be ready to meet the assaulting waves. The inescapable conclusion seems to be that there was a failure to synchronise watches somewhere in the command chain. This failure is unlikely to lie within the brigade since an officer of the 8th Light Horse said that the watches were checked the previous afternoon. Also, Kent Hughes was able to tell Bean that his watch was 'synchronised with all other brigade watches'. To this he added: 'How brigade time was synchronised with other times is a matter for higher command.'[7] Certainly the fault could have been at the divisional level, as he may have been implying.

Perhaps the real explanation is to be found in an innocent comment in the diary of Aubrey Herbert. This officer from Godley's headquarters had played a crucial part in organising and coordinating the armistice to allow for the burial of the dead on 24 May. Obviously it was essential that both sides observe the same timings for the start and conclusion of the truce. It was while arranging this that Herbert noted: 'I found the Turks' time was eight minutes ahead of ours, and put on our watches.'[8]

For some reason there must have been two 'local' times on Gallipoli, eight minutes apart. There was Turkish time and British time. Somehow, and it would not be too remarkable, these sometimes got mixed. If, when he was describing his actions in May, Herbert meant that members of the division's headquarters altered their watches by eight minutes, then he provided an example of how a mix-up may have happened. Without regular time checks, a fundamental action, mistakes could go unnoticed. The eight minutes he mentions is too close to the reported seven minutes pause at The Nek for this explanation to be ignored.

It was the unnecessary waste of life at The Nek that remains the most notorious feature of this battle. Others can be condemned for choosing to attack such an enemy stronghold, but for the devastating losses that ensued Hughes must be held responsible, for such is the burden of command. Where he failed was in the conduct of the action, of which he was in charge, for he was totally out of his depth. No man could comfortably handle the situation which had been presented to him, but in his case he simply had no mental or physical reserves to draw upon. Poor communications compounded his problems, for even after he had given the order to stop some men, obviously unaware of what was happening, still proceeded.

Hughes later said that the attack had not succeeded because he did not get any support. When he wrote to the mother of Captain Rowan, whom he had known when that officer lived in Victoria, to express his sympathy, he said: 'He and his comrades so bravely attempted to take the Turkish trenches. It was one of those heroic acts that failed through want of proper support.'[9] This must have been small consolation to her.

Hughes was right in saying that the level of support that had been expected was not there. However, he still had local command and has to bear responsibility for allowing the attack to continue after the first line had been so decisively defeated and any possibility of success destroyed. Yet Hughes refused to accept any blame. After the war Lieutenant General Sir Talbot Hobbs, a renowned Australian leader who had commanded the Australian division's artillery on Gallipoli, told the official historian:

I remember that General Hughes and Colonel Antill endeavoured to saddle [Johnston's] 2nd F[ield] A[rtillery] Brigade with the responsibility of the disaster, owing they said, to its failure to support or cover the Light Horse attack. I proved ... that these charges were unfounded, and that Colonel [Johnston] was clearly and distinctly ordered to stop firing at 4.30 am.[10]

Hughes's strongest defender was his nephew Wilfrid Kent Hughes. In a letter to the editor of the Melbourne *Argus* in 1924, in which he described himself as 'a minor participant in that attack', he declared that the official historian's published criticisms were unfair and unwarranted. He claimed that the timings and faulty shooting of the artillery were the cause of the disaster, and implied strong criticism of Brazier's actions. He also claimed that Antill was busy carrying out orders and 'could not possibly have found out the true position'.[11]

After the war Hughes responded to the British official historian's account of the action by claiming that he had stopped the attack after the second line went out. He seems to have been unaware, or had forgotten, that there had been four lines, and blamed Brazier for the loss of the third line, 'as the runner was unable to find anyone to deliver the orders to'.[12]

Hughes was neither a fool nor a coward. But he was not a battle-hardened commander and there was nothing in his training or background which could have prepared him for the situation he had to face. He did not even share the experience of previous campaigns with most other officers at his level. Most importantly, the burden of command and the physical exertions of simply holding on at Anzac were too much for a man of his age. When he was a younger and athletic soldier, he had commanded a regiment which, no matter how skilful and dedicated his men, was better prepared for the Crimea than for a modern war. As a peacetime brigade commander, he rarely saw a brigade on the ground, except occasionally at annual encampments, and then he was more concerned with the parade and ceremonial aspects of soldiering. Now, on the battlefield, he was unable to adapt to the circumstances.

It was a noble thing Hughes did when he volunteered to go off to war. But it was his misfortune to be thrown into a situation where quick decisive action was required in the dust and smoke and amid the noise, blood, death and madness of a short and furious battle. Sadly, he did not realise that these things needed to be left to younger men, and should have been content to retire and reflect on his more active days in a time when soldiering meant dashing about in fine uniforms and being presented to Queen Victoria.

When the volume of the Australian official history dealing with the August 1915 battles was published in 1924, the historian's judgement came down heavily against Antill in the account of The Nek action. Charles Bean probably never met Noel Brazier; still he took his evidence at face value and, of course, this weighed heavily against the brigade major. Antill had been opposed to the attack from the start and had, quite correctly, made his opinion known. However, once he had been given his orders he believed that it was his responsibility to carry them out to the letter.

In ordering Brazier to maintain the attack, Antill felt he was properly interpreting Godley's firm instructions, and if there was to be any local departure from these, the orders should come from Hughes. Later he insisted that he bore no responsibility. He said: 'The brigadier was on the spot himself, and if an order were given [to stop], or to be given, it was he, and he alone competent to give it. But no such order was given.'[13] He did not see that in personally dismissing Brazier's appeals he may have been denying Hughes the opportunity, and responsibility, to make an informed decision. The duality in the command, which had been allowed to develop within the brigade, finally had fatal consequences at The Nek.

Antill may not have felt that he was issuing orders, simply restating those which still stood. Brazier provided for the official historian a very descriptive written account of his confrontation with Antill at the head-quarters. At the time the hostility which existed between these two men had prevented any logical discussion. Both times he went to the brigade major he says he was told to 'push on'. This choice of words is significant, as 'push on' was almost the catchcry for the offensive. Godley had insisted that success lay in having his brigades make strong and concentrated efforts. He used these very words in discussing his plans and in giving the orders, and we find them surviving, as one example, in the orders given to Brigadier General Francis Johnston of the New Zealanders. He was told that 'each part of the force must *push on*, whether others were held up or not' (emphasis added).

Antill was also aware that Godley looked poorly on officers who failed to carry out his orders and knew that his future could be at stake. The young dashing mounted officer who had won fame, honours and promotion under fire in South Africa had become, by 1915, rigid and lacking in imagination, and preoccupied with his own career.

It is true that Antill had been in an invidious position, made worse by Hughes' absence. At no time during the action could he see what was happening, and he had to rely upon a few observers' conflicting reports. The first two lines had left so close together that there was no real opportunity of holding the second one back. His fatal decision came when it was the 10th Light Horse's turn to charge. Then he appears to have accepted the demands that the attack proceed without reference to his brigadier.

Clearly Antill had been influenced by the reports of the flag on the parapet. In correspondence with the British war historian, he would later deny any knowledge of the flag, and even seemed to suggest that he regarded this as a story invented by the Australian historian. Bean responded sharply to the comment, saying that he had first been told of the flag by Antill while on Gallipoli.

The courage and sacrifice of the soldiers who went out into the machine-gun fire could not compensate for the inadequacies of command. It is hard to condemn Hughes and Antill for decisions made in such unreasonable circumstances and with the stakes so high. It had been a dangerous, stressful and confusing situation. Still, their decisions were the wrong ones, and while they cannot be blamed for the failure of the attack, they became responsible for the scale of the tragedy.

Following the failed offensive, in October, after further bouts of poor health, Brigadier General Hughes was once again evacuated to hospital with a severe attack of enteric fever.[14] Kent Hughes later noted that this was 'not a light affair for one of his age'.[15] This time he did not return and Antill was appointed to temporarily command the brigade. Birdwood had decided that Hughes was too old to continue and arranged that he be returned to Australia. Antill was duly confirmed in his position and in early 1916 he was promoted to brigadier general. He had managed to serve right through the Gallipoli campaign. 'Anzac was a terrible experience,' he told his brother, 'and I managed – in fact I had to hang on. Fortunately I do not suffer from nerves at all, and it was this nervous strain which blew so many of them out.'[16]

Antill did not remain long with the brigade. The following year his performance in the Sinai, particularly at the battle of Romani, was unremarkable and when a need arose for brigade commanders in France, he was sent there. In the desert he had shown he lacked the ability for quick decisive action, which was often the essence of good mounted work, and it was thought that he might do better with the infantry. Finally, in the mud and cold of the Somme winter, his health gave way. Invalided to England, he was eventually given a training role and did not return to the fighting front again. The luck that had delivered opportunities for him to establish a good reputation in the South African War had deserted him, and he retired from active service a disappointed man.

The command problems at The Nek had been compounded by the deaths of Lieutenant Colonels White and Miell, the regimental commanding officers, and possibly by the absence of the experienced Captain MacFarlane, who had gone away wounded some weeks earlier. Had they been there to call upon Hughes or Antill to stop the attack, things may have been different. As it was, there was only Brazier, who had to go to Antill, and there could not have been a worse combination. In the eyes of Hughes and Antill, Brazier had lost all credibility. To them it was hardly remarkable that he should query the orders, as he had often done so in the past. Brazier was contemptuous of both the senior officers, as they were of him. He was correct on this occasion, but his opinion carried no weight.

Lieutenant Colonel White's decision to lead his men was typical of the man. Judged against the simple rule that you should not ask your men to do anything that you would not do, it was a noble gesture. But it was a fatal mistake. White's death in the first few moments left his regiment without its commanding officer. One can only wonder what might have happened if, after seeing his first line shot down, he had been there to order the remaining men to stand fast.

Brazier's actions were correct ones for a commanding officer. Having seen two lines destroyed, and with no chance of success left, there could be no reason for the remaining lines to go out. However, his own earlier actions had contributed to the lack of confidence in which he was held. Error turned to confusion when it became necessary for him to run around looking for Hughes. It meant that he also could not be found when his own officers sought him out for further orders. This confusion probably contributed to the loss of part of the fourth line.

The role of the staff officers who were to indicate the time for each line to leave the trenches is not clear. It appears that they never received the orders to stop the attack, at least until after the third line had gone out. Lieutenant Kent Hughes was one of them. Evidently The Nek was one of the low points in his otherwise distinguished military service during two world wars. When Bean was trying to piece together the events of that day after the war, he found Hughes uncooperative. Many years later, in conversation with Ian Fitchett, a political journalist and former war correspondent, Kent Hughes denied having been at The Nek. Perhaps, being an astute politician, he simply wanted to be rid of a journalist and distance himself from being identified with a disaster. But even as an old man he would not provide any assistance to historian Bill Gammage, who was seeking information about the attack.

An interesting sidelight to Kent Hughes' contact with Charles Bean is worth relating. He was clearly not happy with Bean's account of the battle in the official history. Naturally, it reflected poorly on his uncle, of whom he was very fond. In the course of his defence of his uncle, Kent Hughes asked Bean to give the sources for some of his statements. Bean wrote back sharply: 'You cannot be serious in expecting me to disclose to you the names of those living persons on whose statements this story is based.'[17] Kent Hughes could hardly have been pleased with this reply. As events unfolded, it was Kent Hughes who eventually became the minister responsible for the Australian War Memorial and the writing of the official history of the Second World War. In this more recent conflict Kent Hughes had been an officer in the 8th Australian division and was a supporter of Lieutenant General Gordon Bennett, who had commanded the division before he escaped to Australia after the surrender of Singapore. Kent Hughes, suspicious as he now was of official war historians, gave Gavin Long – Bean's Second World War counterpart – a harrowing time during the preparation of the account of that controversial episode.

The other staff officer, Kenneth McKenzie, kept a diary on Gallipoli, but his brief entries reveal very few of his personal thoughts of this time. He says nothing of his and Kent Hughes's role on 7 August, and only ponders why the artillery did not fire throughout the attack. Major Reynell's part during the action is hard to assess. He seems to have been the wild card, urging Antill to press the attack at the same time that Brazier was trying to stop it.

It was inevitable that the consequences of the lack of battle experience would emerge in the brigade's first large offensive effort. They knew little of what to expect once they were out of the trenches. The officers and NCOs were equally raw, most of them holding their positions because of their peacetime ranks and social positions. Reynell, White, Anderson, Dale, Piesse and Turnbull, together with several others, might have gone on to become outstanding leaders had they not perished in the August fighting. Lieutenant Colonel White had made a good early impression, but his resolve to lead from the front was possibly the worst decision in the whole misadventure.

The campaign at Anzac ended in December with the British and empire troops evacuating quietly, undetected by the Turks. The allies had to console themselves that at least the evacuation was well-planned and well-executed. The light horsemen went back to Egypt and to their horses. Some officers and men transferred to other units, and a few fought on the Western Front.

For the rest of the war the 3rd Light Horse Brigade served as a mounted formation in the campaigns in the Sinai and Palestine, and these operations took a further toll on the small band of Nek survivors. Bad luck continued to dog the 8th Regiment; it would lose another famous commanding officer, Leslie Maygar, a holder of the Victoria Cross, in action in 1917. With a record of misfortune, it seems hardly surprising that the first light horseman killed in the new theatre of war, Corporal Stephen Monaghan, who died on 13 April 1916, was one of that regiment's Nek veterans. It seemed so unfair that a man could survive the hail of bullets at The Nek only to die in an isolated skirmish. The Nek survivors held a special place in the unit and Monaghan's death was bitterly felt, as a comment by one of the officers shows: 'Monaghan ... took part in the famous charge of the 8th LH and was one of ten who escaped uninjured; then to come out here in order to be picked off in a rotten little scrap.'[18]

Throughout the war the losses had been high among the officers. In the end, Andy Crawford was the only one of the original group who had left in early 1915 to return home in his regiment. At The Nek the 9th Light Horse had been spared the many casualties of its sister regiments, although the deaths of Miell, and then Reynell a few weeks later, were a shock for the South Australians – made all the worse because Frank Rowell, who commanded the state's other regiment, died in the same month. To lose three light horse commanding officers, all leading citizens, was a sharp reminder that in this war death was no respecter of rank.

Joe Scott took over the 10th Light Horse after Brazier's departure but was blown to pieces by a shell several weeks later. Tom Todd returned to Anzac to be appointed to the command and led the regiment for the rest of the war. He became one of the most respected officers of the Australian Light Horse and continued to serve, despite being severely wounded during 1917 in the second battle of Gaza. Two survivors of The Nek battle rose to command their regiments: McLaurin of the 8th Regiment and Todd of the 10th. By a sad coincidence both got through the war only to die from illnesses before they could return to Australia.

CHAPTER 14

Remembrance

The waste of life at The Nek in many ways epitomises the First World War. After Gallipoli the AIF would be presented with further impossible tasks, and again determination and courage would not prevent tragedy or defeats. The losses became part of Australia's continuing and mounting 'roll of honour'. At Fromelles and Bullecourt in France, and at the third battle of Ypres in Belgium, the losses were on a vastly greater scale. At Fromelles, on 19 July 1916, an Australian division attacked and was repulsed by the Germans for the loss of 5500 casualties. Yet even when compared against these big battles, The Nek is still remembered for its total futility.

Those who survived the war returned home to try to take up life where they had left off. Many succeeded. Others were invalids or bore mental scars from their experiences; they and their families sometimes suffered decades of torment. The veterans – they were called 'returned men' back then – retained a common bond and were a visible part of the population for a further half century. They were never more visible than on Anzac Day each year, when many of them would assemble wearing their medals, to march once again under banners announcing the names of their proud units. But time slowly overcame them until none was left. Lionel Simpson, the last known living survivor of the charge, died in 1991 aged 100.[1]

Frederic Hughes lived a long and full life until his death in 1944. After the war he returned to his business affairs, his interest in the turf, and his military club. At the club he was remembered as 'an attractive conversationalist and with advancing years, he did not commit that intolerable and yet widespread social sin of becoming either a "club bore" or a "Colonel Blimp"'.[2]

Antill returned to a military post in Australia. He was in New South Wales for a short time, then in 1918 he was appointed Commandant in

South Australia. In an interesting twist of fate, he was there in August 1919 to accept the salute of the 9th Light Horse on the regiment's return from the war. It had been five years since he had been introduced to the unit amid some controversy, but it must have seemed a lifetime. This time he complimented the men on their smart appearance and steadiness. He had been appointed CMG for his war service, and in 1924 he finally retired from the army with the rank of major general.

As an old man Antill bore his disappointments quietly, although he was clearly angered by the Australian and British official historians' accounts of his actions on Gallipoli. He once told his daughter: 'Keep your chin up. Have no regrets. Life is made up of disappointment.'³ She must have been aware that controversy had surrounded his public and private life, but claimed that 'he cared so little for praise or blame'. In his last years he had few close friends but remained active and alert and involved himself in many interests. He retained his enthusiasm for the theatre and with his daughter, Rose Antill de Warren, drew on his family's history to help write a three-part drama, *The Emancipist*, which was published in 1936. But he was already a sick man; he died of cancer on 1 March 1937.

The tragedy of war was again visited on the families of some of the central characters of The Nek saga. Reynell's only son was killed in 1940 while serving with the Royal Air Force. Like White's son, Alexander, Richard Reynell had grown up with pride in the memory of his brave father but sorrow in not having known him. In the Second World War Alexander White was a medical officer in the 8th Australian Division in Malaya. Elsewhere in this division was Brazier's son, Arthur, who was a member of Western Australia's 2/4th Machine Gun Battalion. Both men became prisoners of war of the Japanese following the surrender of Singapore. White survived, but Brazier died in captivity in 1943. His father lived long enough to receive the news of his loss: war had dealt him another bitter blow.

Noel Brazier lived out his life on his property, part of which was broken up for soldier-settlement. A neighbour recalled: 'Although socially they mixed very little in the district, the Brazier family, like all the established farmers, were very supportive of the Returned Soldier Settlers. The colonel was an aloof man, but his wife was a beautiful and gracious lady, always a leader in any scheme to improve conditions in the district.'⁴ In his later years Brazier remained outspoken and sometimes wrote to the newspapers on matters as diverse as politics, local government and even road manners. He died at his home in September 1947.

After the war Charles Bean spent the next two decades writing his history of the AIF's exploits. As soon as he could after peace came, he went back to Turkey to walk the abandoned battlefields of Gallipoli. Among those accompanying him on the 1919 Historical Mission were George Lambert the artist and Hubert Wilkins the famous explorer and photographer. Bean wanted to go to familiar places once more to see the battlefields from the Turkish viewpoint, and to solve what he called 'the riddles of Anzac'. It was an important opportunity for him as a historian and provided a last chance to obtain some relics from the campaign for display back in Australia. Lambert and Wilkins were each required to produce a visual record of the former battlefields.

George Washington Lambert had made his impact as a painter in Australia almost 20 years before the war. He had been living in Britain when war broke out and, in November 1917, he was approached by the Australian government to record some of the work of the AIF. Even while the fighting was still in progress, Bean had formed some ideas for a war memorial museum to be established in Australia as an enduring record of the AIF's part in the Great War. Now on Gallipoli he discussed with Lambert his wish for two large paintings. One would depict the landing of the Anzacs on 25 April 1915, and the other the charge at The Nek. These paintings would be done later, but the visit to Gallipoli enabled Lambert to study the battle site, its surroundings, and even the morning light.

Bean and Lambert climbed up to The Nek on the first day of the Historical Mission's visit. Lambert was to say that 'for the point of view of the artist-historian The Neck [*sic*] is a wonderful setting to the tragedy'.[5] Eventually, the loneliness of the whole area, and the remains of so many dead to which teams of war graves personnel were attending, affected Bean and Lambert, and both men were relieved to finally leave in early March on the first stage of their separate journeys back to Australia.

Lambert's large and graphic painting *The charge of the 3rd Light Horse Brigade at The Nek* was completed for the Australian War Memorial Museum in 1925. This museum, which exhibited in Melbourne and Sydney, was the beginning of Bean's dream, which culminated in the opening of the Australian War Memorial in Canberra in 1941. In Sydney the museum's guidebook drew visitors' attention to the newly installed painting, and to a soldier's nearby haversack ('shot through and through') which Bean had collected from the site of the battle. The charge was described in the book as 'that wonderful episode in our country's history'.[6]

When Charles Bean and his party walked over the old battle site in 1919, it was still littered with the scattered bones and other grisly remains of the dead, abandoned when the allied troops had evacuated four years earlier. They also saw that the Turks had erected a monument to commemorate their efforts in resisting the invader. The place which had been a critical objective throughout the campaign had become one of historical and symbolic importance to both Australians and Turks.

It had already been determined that the empire's war dead would be honoured by proper burials and that the missing would be commemorated with their names on memorials. In accordance with the Imperial War Graves Commission's decision concerning the handling of the Gallipoli soldiers' graves, most of the Australians were buried near where their remains lay rather than being concentrated in one or two large cemeteries. And so graves were made at The Nek and the pathetic remnants of more than 300 men were buried between the old opposing lines. Only ten of these men could be given names.[7] At Lone Pine a large memorial was built, and here the names of all those whose bodies could not be found or identified were inscribed. Of the 427 names of the missing officers and men of the light horse regiments recorded on the memorial, 161 belong to the 8th Light Horse.

The Nek cemetery is a flat grassed regular plot measuring 25 x 33 metres, contained within a low stone wall. At the head of the plot is a short raised wall embossed with a Christian cross. Within the cemetery there are only five identified graves under a row of modest flat headstones. Another five headstones record graves of men whose exact locations in the cemetery are not known.

One of the sparse headstones bears the name of Trooper Geoffrey Howell, whose mate in the 10th Light Horse later recalled the awfulness of his death. The two men had made the charge from the trench and lay out in no-man's-land under intense fire. 'I heard someone calling me and discovered it was Jeff Howell, a particular chum of mine,' wrote Sergeant 'Matie' Hoops. 'He desired me to shoot him as he said he was settled. It was a rare sight to see the smile on his face all the time – I will never forget it. Poor fellow, he got a bullet through the head a little later.'[8]

The Nek cemetery looks almost empty as the remaining 316 burials lie unmarked in six rows beneath the grass. There are those of Australians and New Zealanders, some of whose deaths date back to the first days of the fighting. However, the majority are of men of the 8th and 10th Light Horse Regiments who were killed on 7 August. The plot is screened on one side by cypress trees, pines and coarse scrub. Only a few metres away traces of old trenches and evidence of collapsed tunnels are still to be found.

Adjoining the Australian cemetery is the Turkish memorial. Following the defeat of the invader, the Turks erected three monuments at Anzac to celebrate their victory. That at The Nek is the only original one remaining, although new monuments have been constructed at various sites. Known as Sergeant Mehmet's Memorial (Mehmet Çavuş Anıtı), it has become a focus for Turkish commemoration. It is in the form of a monolith and has been improved and enclosed in more recent times, with only the base being retained from the old wartime monument.

It is said that Sergeant Mehmet fought here in the first few days of the campaign, until his death. He is said to have cried 'I die happily for my country, and you, my comrades, will avenge me.'⁹ Whether the sergeant was real or mythical is less important than the role he fulfils today by representing the ordinary Turkish soldiers' deeds and sacrifice.

Viewed from far away the old battlefield may not seem to have changed much since the young soldiers of two nations faced each other across this narrow patch of land high on a Turkish coastal ridge. But seen closer up, it is quite different from when it was heavily scarred with trenches and saps. The men of both sides suffered equally, and this was a place of brave deeds and tragedy for all. When the invaders went away, the trenches and tunnels were abandoned. The remains of the dead lay littered about until 1919, even while the victors were building their monument. Eventually, the terrible smell, remembered with horror by the soldiers, was swept away by sea breezes, the trenches crumbled and filled leaving only shallow traces, while the combatants went off to face an uncertain future.

In Australia the action at The Nek has been depicted in paintings, literature and film. It has been described in fact and in fiction. Bean gave a detailed reconstruction in the official history and Lambert had made it the subject of one of his most famous war paintings.

In 1981 interest in The Nek was revived by the release of the Australian film *Gallipoli*. The film appeared at a strange time. The Vietnam War and the divisions that it had created within the community were still fresh in the public's mind and old war stories did not seem to be much in demand.

Gallipoli was a product of the imagination of Peter Weir, then a young director who, in the previous half dozen years, had established a reputation with a number of visually stimulating and thought-provoking movies. Weir had visited Gallipoli five years earlier and was haunted by what he found. He also drew inspiration from Bean's writing and from the work of Bill Gammage, a historian who had brought a fresh approach to war history by drawing on preserved accounts of individual's experiences. Gammage assisted in the production of the film, and the screenplay was written by David Williamson.

Gallipoli reached an enormous Australian audience, was distributed overseas and was even shown in Turkey. Today many Australians draw their images of the 1915 campaign from Weir's influential film. In the final climactic scene the story's hero, young Archie Hamilton from Western Australia, is shown running across no-man's-land. In the words of the screenplay: 'he has dropped his rifle and is sprinting his last race. Inevitably he is hit by a machine-gun blast but it appears as though he has just breasted an invisible tape.' Weir captured the same fatal moment that George Lambert had presented in his painting.

For a brief time in 1990 the Gallipoli battles again came to local and international attention when some of the old adversaries joined together to mark the 75th anniversary of the campaign. In a remarkable exercise, the Australian government was able to gather together a band of aged veterans to take them back to the small coastal strip in Turkey where they had once risked their lives and lost their youth. Australia watched emotionally as these men, representatives of a vanishing generation, received their salute. From that time on, large numbers of Australians have gone to Gallipoli to mark Anzac Day each year. The last Anzac died in 2002, more than a decade after the passing of the last man to have survived the charge at The Nek.

Despite the passage of time, changing perceptions and the disappearance of the veterans, the Anzac story remains an enduring Australian legend. The charge at The Nek is a central component of this story. It possesses a grand heroic quality, despite also being a testament to the tragedy of war and a reminder of the terrible cost in human lives upon which military legends are built.

Roll of Honour

8th Light Horse

Buried in The Nek Cemetery

857 Tpr H.E. Stanley

Buried in Walker's Ridge Cemetery

... Major T.H. Redford

Buried in Ari Burnu Cemetery

678 Tpr F.L. A'Beckett
801 " A.A. Anderson
235 L Cpl J.A. Anderson
... Lieut L.W.H. Anderson
806 Tpr P. Beckett
338 " V.E. Blakeney
693 " T.A. Dudderidge
692 " T.L. Dwyer
... Lieut E.E. Henty
542 Tpr A.H. Moreton
325 " A. Nicolson
551 " W. Tosh
184 " J.G.F. Thompson
22 " C.H. Walsh

No known grave

755 Tpr J.V. Airey
682 " R.S. Alban
756 " R.O. Alexander
607 " P.J. Amor

544 " G.J.S. Anderson
608 " W.S. Anderson
876 " S. Arbuthnot
881 " W.E. Barton
527 " R. Beilby
878 " J.A. Bell
601 " C. Benson
234 Cpl A.D. Bethune
805 Tpr D. Boddy
46 Sgt H. Bohlsen
... Lieut K. Bothwick
209 L Cpl J. Boswell
880 Tpr R. Bowering
233 Cpl A.S. Bowker
342 Dvr W. Burke
311 Tpr M.A. Cakebread
300 Sgt Maj C.H. Cameron
686 Tpr J.P. Cameron
853 " J.M. Carney
59 " A.E. Carpenter
... Lieut C. Carthew
129 L Cpl A. Cavanagh
281 Tpr N. Clayton
776 " T.G. Coates
689 " W. Combs
115 Sgt J.L. Connor
151 Tpr J. Considine

240	”	J. Conway	168	”	J. Hay
70	Cpl	H. Cowell	247	”	B. Hill
534	Tpr	C.H. Cramond	213	”	W.A. Hind
58	Dvr	A.G. Cumming	200	Cpl	R.G. Hindhaugh
884	Cpl	H.R. Currie	623	Tpr	G.R. Hope
…	Lieut	C.C. Dale	897	”	H. Hoskins
694	Tpr	P.G. Dewhurst	…	Lieut	T.S. Howard
89	”	O.E. Donaldson	201	L Cpl	G.T. Hughes
781	”	W. Dow	742	Tpr	S. James
690	”	A. Driscoll	229	”	D. Jamieson
662	”	J. Duffy	217	”	D.M.M. Johnson
702	”	A.S. Dunn	316	L Cpl	J.J. Jolly
		(served as Palmer)	828	Tpr	A. Jones
817	”	S. Edmiston	394	”	T. Jones
618	”	W. Essay	547	”	F.W. Kemp
369	”	A.L. Evans	400	”	R. Kerr
368	”	A.G. Evans	831	”	M.F. King
889	”	H.E. Eyers	83	”	A.B. Kinnaird
212	”	L.G. Finn	251	”	A.R. Knight
821	”	B. Forbes	898	”	W. Lang
265	Sgt	T.C. Forde	762	”	M.E. Larkin
158	Tpr	A.W. Fyffe	834	”	R. Lees
245	”	W.H. Gale	133	”	H. Lennon
824	”	E.B. Gibbs	132	”	T. Longmore
893	Cpl	H.G. Gordon	906	”	C.R. McAnally
286	Tpr	E.S. Goulden	744	”	H. McCarthy
287	”	J.G.L. Goyne	263	”	S.J. McColl
709	Cpl	H. Grace	177	”	W.A. McElhinney
894	Tpr	G.L. Graham	…	2/Lieut	C.G. Marsh
929	”	G.T. Grant	255	Tpr	R. Martin
…	Lieut	G.M. Grant	903	”	O.J. Matthies
381	Sgt	C. Grenfell	254	”	R.R. Mitchell
698	Tpr	L.G. Griffin	414	”	W. Mitchell
621	”	M.D. Griffiths	138	”	J.E. Moysey
760	”	F.G. Hall	766	”	T.R. Murray
250	”	R.D. Harris	142	”	W.E. Newton
896	”	J. Hastings	554	”	B.L. O'Mullane

432	Sgt	S.J. O'Neill
264	Tpr	G.B. Ormerod
41	Sgt	R. Palmer
910	Tpr	R.W. Patterson
232	Sgt	J.B. Pickett
746	Tpr	A. Preece
482	L Cpl	G. Purves
198	Cpl	V.N. Raymond
850	Tpr	R.W. Richardson
		(served as Wallace)
42	Sgt	H.G. Roberts
715	Tpr	F. Roderick
913	"	E.L. Shearsmith
453	"	H.S. Sheldon
750	"	A.J. Stanford
919	"	G. Stenzel
643	"	J.A. Stewart
296	"	C.T. Sutherland
841	"	P.J. Sweeney
858	"	N. Tackaberry
75	"	S.H. Taylor
923	"	W. Toleman
752	"	A.D. Trewin
150	"	V.K. Walton
298	L Cpl	J.F. Weatherhead
784	Tpr	W.B. Welch
...	Lt Col	A.H. White
...	2/Lieut	E. Whitehead

261	Tpr	A.S. Williams
475	Dvr	R. Williamson
...	Lieut	E.G. Wilson
729	Tpr	J.J. Wilson
225	"	C.M. Wingrove
333	Tpr	J. Winnett
...	Lieut	C.T. Woods

Died and buried at sea between 7 and 12 August 1915

156	Tpr	D.F. Cole
304	L Cpl	A.N. Tetley
327	Tpr	F. Payne
130	"	C. Kelly
160	"	F.G. Gipps
155	"	L.W. Cole
559	"	C. Greaves
541	"	E.P. Hendy
663	"	P. Morrisey
167	"	A.H. Griffiths
314	"	C. Holmberg
532	"	R. Willan

Died of wounds Egypt/Malta/Mudros

208	Tpr	J.H. Baker
182	Tpr	J. Shaw
722	Tpr	R. Somerville

10th Light Horse

Buried in The Nek Cemetery

803	Tpr	R. Howell
96	"	G.C. Howell
966	"	E. Penny

Buried in Walker's Ridge Cemetery

962	Tpr	D.S. McLean
631	"	H. Pope
152	"	H. Rush
898	"	C.E. Sutton

Buried in Ari Burnu Cemetery

364	Sgt	D.F.G. Bain
97	L Cpl	L.L.S. Chipper
68	Tpr	R.R.V. Chipper
93	"	T. Combley
139	"	R.E. Cumming
153	"	J.C. Eyre
403	Cpl	R.A. Forbes
828	Tpr	A. Hancock
735	"	H.G. McNeill
80	"	W.R.E. Northey
741	"	L.P. Payne
325	"	A.A. Pearson
231	Sgt	F.A. Rawlings
333	Tpr	C.A. Robinson
…	2/Lieut	L.J.C. Roskams
…	Capt	A.P. Rowan
212	SSM	J. Springall
…	2/Lieut	A.P. Turnbull
357	Tpr	F.H. Weston

Buried in Shrapnel Valley Cemetery

372	Tpr	W. Blake
33	"	W.H. Lailey

No known grave

101	Tpr	W.F. Anderson
778	"	J. Anderson
103	"	H. Barraclough
934	"	H. Bower
709	"	E.V. Brady
69	"	H.H. Brockman
379	"	F.J. Bunce
165	L Cpl	T.F. Burges
712	Tpr	A.J. Butler
937	"	P.J. Cameron
860	"	H.T. Chipper
142	"	A.G. Cobb
787	"	H.A. Collins
718	"	R.D. Davis
791	"	G.E. DeMole
539	"	R.G. Dempster
166	"	A.L. Doust
394	Cpl	D. DuVal
84	Tpr	N.C. Dyer
1804	Tpr	W.W. Eustace
109	Sgt	B.M. Fenwick
521	Tpr	J. Flux
728	"	W. Hahn
113	"	G. Harper
114	"	W.L. Harper
112	"	O.D.H. Hassell
…	Lieut	T.J. Heller
292	Tpr	H. Hill
…	Lieut	D.A. Jackson
141	Tpr	F.W. Kirsch
150	"	L.A. Klopper
120	"	J.P. Lewis
116	"	D. Lukin
307	"	W.H. Mason
170	Sgt	E. McAliece
450	L Cpl	A.J. McClusky
123	Tpr	J.B. McJannett
813	"	W.C. McKenzie
…	Capt	R.T. McMasters
125	Tpr	G. McRae
138	Sgt	R.J. Moore
…	Capt	V.F. Piesse
125	Tpr	A.T. Pitts
331	Tpr	A. Rae
82	"	G.W. Richardson
130	"	W.A. Ross
891	"	G.F.H. Sandy
226	Sgt	J.A. Scott

157	Cpl	C. Shepherd
147	Tpr	W.J. Snudden
902	"	O.S. Timms
748	"	L. Villis
143	"	E.J. White

Buried Baby 700 Cemetery

| 821 | Cpl | T. Thompson |
| 71 | Tpr | J. Wilkerson |

Died of wounds, Egypt

| 526 | Tpr | A. Gannaway |

Died of wounds, Malta

| 79 | Tpr | F.W. Scrivens |

Buried at sea, 10 August 1915

224	Tpr	T. Buckingham
283	"	H. G. Hill
409	Sgt	J. A. Gollan

9th Light Horse

Buried in Ari Burnu Cemetery

361	SSM	W.E. Harvey
...	Lt Col	A. Miell
62	L Cpl	G.R. Seager
746	Tpr	F.J. Smith

Died and buried at sea

| 542 | Tpr | F.N. Drew |

No official list of casualties at The Nek has been found. These names have been compiled from the regular AIF casualty reports and confirmed against war graves and memorial registers. The Official History figures (given as 8th Light Horse, 12 officers and 142 men; 10th Light Horse 7 officers and 73 men) are slightly understated by evidently not including men who died while being evacuated as casualties.

NOTES

Chapter 1: The Attack at The Nek

1 H.J. Nugent, letter to mother, unattributed newspaper cutting (author's copy)
2 C.E.W. Bean, *The Story of Anzac from 4 May, 1915, to the Evacuation of the Gallipoli Peninsula*, vol. 2: Official History of Australia in the War of 1914–1918, Angus and Robertson, Sydney, 1924, p. 633
3 C.E.W. Bean, *The Australian Imperial Force in France during the Allied Offensive*, Vol. 6: Official History of Australia in the War of 1914–1918, Angus and Robertson, Sydney, 1942, p. 1083
4 J.L. Treloar (ed.), *Australian Chivalry: Reproductions in colour and duo-tone of official war paintings*, Australian War Memorial, Canberra, 1945, p. 13

Chapter 2: 3rd Light Horse Brigade

1 W.A. McConnan, letter to father, 14 September 1914. Papers held by Miss N.M. McConnan, South Yarra, Vic.
2 Peter Burness, 'Tragedy of two brothers', *Wartime* 54, April 2011, p. 56. (From papers held by Mrs. N. Titchener, Seacliff Park, SA)
3 (Lieutenant Colonel) A.H. White, diary. Papers held by Mrs M. McPherson, Bulleen, Victoria
4 McConnan, letter to father, 15 November 1914. AWM PR01577
5 Interview with H.D. Dean of Ballarat, Victoria, Canberra, 20 August 1984
6 C. Reynell, diary, 19 December 1914. AWM PR86/388

Chapter 3: The Brigadier

1 Alf Batchelder, 'Sport and war', *The Yorker*, Journal of the Melbourne Cricket Club Library, no. 41, Autumn 2010, p. 4
2 R.K. Peacock, 'Some Australian gunners of last century', *As You Were, 1946*, Australian War Memorial, Canberra, 1951, p. 121
3 John Butler Cooper, *The History of St Kilda: From its first settlement to a city and after, 1840–1930*, Printers Proprietary Ltd, Melbourne, 1931, vol. 2, p. 246
4 *Australian Dictionary of Biography*, vol. 9, Melbourne University Press, Carlton, Vic., 1983, p. 388
5 Lindsay C. Cox, *The Galloping Guns of Rupertswood and Werribee Park: A history of the Victorian Horse*, Coonans Hills Press, Pascoe Vale South, Vic., 1986, p. 22
6 Cooper, *The History of St. Kilda,* vol. 2, p. 11
7 Frederick Howard, *Kent Hughes: A biography of Colonel The Hon. Sir Wilfrid Kent Hughes*, Macmillan, South Melbourne, 1972, p. 10
8 W. Perry, 'The Victorian Horse Artillery', *The Victorian Historical Magazine*, vol. 43, no. 1, p. 754
9 Howard, *Kent Hughes,* p. 10

10 W. Robinson, letter to official historian, 16 May 1924. Records of C.E.W. Bean, AWM 38 3DRL 8042 Item 25

11 11th Australian Light Horse, Regimental Order No. 16, 14 May 1906. AWM 1 Item 18/4

12 Cooper, *The History of St. Kilda*, vol. 2, p. 246

13 Melbourne *Argus*, 13 January 1915

14 Record of Service Book (Staff Corps). AWM 182 (1A), p. 137

Chapter 4: The Brigade Major

1 R.L. Wallace, *The Australians at the Boer War*, Australian War Memorial, Canberra, 1976, p. 134

2 Later General Sir Beauvoir de Lisle, a British cavalry officer with a fierce reputation who later commanded the British 29th Division on Gallipoli and the Western Front.

3 New South Wales Military Forces, General Order No. 141, 10 October 1900, Government Printer, Sydney

4 Alderson was a British infantry officer who was an exponent of mounted infantry. He later commanded the Canadian Corps for a period during the First World War.

5 P.L. Murray (ed.), *Official Records of the Australian Military Contingents to the War in South Africa*, Government Printer, Melbourne, 1911, p. 31

6 R.V. Pockley, *Ancestor Treasure Hunt: The Edward Wills family and descendants in Australia, 1797–1976*, Wentworth Books, Sydney, 1978, p. 102

7 *Melbourne Punch*, 25 February 1915, p. 256

8 Interview with C. Newman (former light horse officer), Canberra, 3 July 1979

9 Richard Williams, *These Are Facts: The autobiography of Air Marshal Sir Richard Williams KBE CB DSO*, Australian War Memorial, Canberra, 1977, p. 13

10 Keith Isaacs, *Military Aircraft of Australia, 1909–1918*, Australian War Memorial, Canberra, 1971, p. 9

11 Commonwealth of Australia, Military Board Proceedings 1915, Agenda, pp. 179–84. National Archives of Australia, A2653

12 Ruth Crutchfield (daughter), quoted in Pockley, *Ancestor Treasure Hunt*, p. 104

13 *The Kia Ora Coo-ee*, 15 September 1918, p. 12

14 Edmond Samuels, *If the Cap Fits*, Modern Literature Co., Sydney, 1972, p. 37

15 *Northern Star* (Lismore), 17 September 1912

16 J. Antill, letter to wife, 1 October 1912, NSW State Archives, Divorce Case Papers, Divorce 96 of 1912

17 C.E.W. Bean, *The Story of Anzac from the Outbreak of War to the End of the First Phase of the Gallipoli Campaign, May 4, 1915*, vol. 1: Official History of Australia in the War of 1914–1918, Angus and Robertson, Sydney, 1938, p. 138

18 *Sydney Mail*, 30 September 1914

19 E. Scott, *Australia During the War*, vol. 11: Official History of Australia in the War of 1914–1918, Angus and Robertson, Sydney, 1939, p. 160

Chapter 5: Officers and Men

1 Colin S. Fraser and Raymond E. Mahlook, *The History of Joe White Maltings Limited 1858–1989*, Joe White Maltings, Collingwood, 1991, p. 13

2 (A.H. White) Mrs M.L. McMinn, letter to C.E.W. Bean, 12 May 1924. AWM 43 Official history, 1914–18 War, Biographical and other research files

3 A.H. White, papers held by Mrs M. McPherson, Bulleen, Vic.

4 Interview with H.D. Dean, of Ballarat, Victoria. Canberra, 20 August 1984

5 Interview with L. Simpson, of Bacchus Marsh, Victoria. Canberra, 20 August 1984

6 A. Crawford, '3rd L.H. Bde. on Gallipoli', *Reveille*, 1 August 1932, p. 38

7 Alan Parker, 'WA's Harness Heritage', *Wes-Trot*, January 1997, p. 32

8 Descended from the former Western Australian Mounted Rifles, the regiment was at that time called the 18th Australian Light Horse, but the name would change to the 25th Light Horse in 1912.

9 A.C.N. Olden, *Westralian Cavalry in the War: The story of the Tenth Light Horse Regiment, AIF, in the Great War, 1914–1918* , Alexander McCubbin, Melbourne, 1921, p. 12

10 Captain A.M. Ross, letter to Captain C.S. Davies, 6 June 1915, *RMC Journal*, Bateson and Co., Sydney, 1915. p. 20

11 C.E.W. Bean, *The Story of Anzac from the Outbreak of War to the End of the First Phase of the Gallipoli Campaign, May 4, 1915*, vol. 1: Official History of Australia in the War of 1914–1918, Angus and Robertson, Sydney, 1938, p. 60

12 Suzanne Welborn, *Lords of Death: A people, a place, a legend*, Fremantle Arts Centre Press, Fremantle, 1982, p. 190

13 Quoted in John Rickard, *H.B. Higgins: The rebel as judge*, George Allen and Unwin, Sydney, 1984, p. 207

14 Rickard, *H.B. Higgins*, p. 216

15 Royal Military College, Sandhurst, UK, Letter to author from archivist, 22 January 1991

16 Extracted from embarkation rolls (original squadrons). AWM 8, 1914–18 War, Item 10/15/1

17 Reynell, diary, 27 February 1915. AWM PR86/388

18 T.H. Darley, *With the Ninth Light Horse in the Great War*, Hassell Press, Adelaide, 1924, p. 12

19 H.S. Gullett, *The Australian Imperial Force in Sinai and Palestine, 1914–1918*, vol. 7: Official History of Australia in the War of 1914–1918, Angus and Robertson, Sydney, 1941, p. 38

20 Margaret Kiddle, *Men of Yesterday: A social history of the Western District of Victoria, 1834–1890*, Melbourne University Press, Melbourne, 1967, p. 14

21 *Hamilton Spectator*, 20 August 1915

22 Interview with H.D. Dean, August 1984, Canberra

23 Melbourne *Argus*, 13 January 1915

24 Adelaide *Advertiser*, 16 November 1914

25 Adelaide *Advertiser*, 16 January 1915

26 Adelaide, *The Register*, 14 November 1914

27 *Melbourne Punch*, 25 February 1915, p. 256

28 Melbourne *Herald*, 20 January 1915

Chapter 6: Egypt

1 T.S. Austin, 'History of the 8th ALH Regiment'. AWM MSS0351

2 Austin, 'History of the 8th ALH Regiment'

3 N. Brazier, diary, 19 February 1915. AWM 1 DRL 147

4 A.H. White, diary. Papers held by Mrs. M. McPherson, Bulleen, Victoria.

5 C. Reynell, diary, entry for 28 February 1915. AWM PR86/388

6 *Australian Dictionary of Biography*, vol. 11, Melbourne University Press, Carlton, Vic., 1988, pp. 366–67

7 J. Antill, diary, entry for 30 August 1915. AWM 3DRL 6458

8 Brazier, papers

9 White, diary
10 John Rickard, *H.B. Higgins, the Rebel as Judge*, Allen and Unwin, Sydney, 1984, p. 220
11 W.A. McConnan, letter to father, 7 April 1915. AWM PR01577
12 White, diary
13 Quoted in Frederick Howard, *Kent Hughes: A biography of Colonel The Hon. Sir Wilfrid Kent Hughes*, Macmillan, South Melbourne, 1972, p. 14
14 McConnan papers, letter to sister, 25–27 April 1915
15 White, diary
16 Campbell diary, entry for 5 May 1915. AWM PR88/102
17 White, diary
18 Antill, papers. AWM 3DRL 6458
19 Brazier, papers
20 Brazier, papers
21 McConnan, letter to father, 4 May 1915
22 White, papers
23 H. Foss, diary. AWM 1 DRL 298. The nickname 'Go Alone' evidently derived from Brazier's declaration in Australia that if the regiment did not buckle down to training he would go alone.
24 N. Brazier, diary, 16 May 1915

Chapter 7: Gallipoli and Trench Warfare

1 C. Reynell, diary, entry for 17 May 1915. AWM PR86/388
2 H. Foss, diary. AWM 1DRL 298. After serving on Gallipoli, Foss eventually became a stowaway to get to France with the infantry, where he was killed, after having been commissioned, in 1917.
3 Reynell, diary, entry for 22 May 1915
4 A.H. White, diary
5 T.A. Kidd, diary. AWM PR82/137
6 Kidd, diary
7 A.H. White, diary. Papers held by Mrs M. McPherson, Bulleen, Victoria
8 W. Cameron, diary. AWM 1DRL 185
9 Reynell, diary, entry for 25 May 1915
10 Kidd, diary
11 Kidd, diary
12 Kidd, diary
13 Interview with H.D. Dean, Canberra, 20 August 1984
14 Foss, diary
15 W. McConnan, letter to father, 17 October 1915
16 White, diary
17 Cameron, diary. This is also the source of the next three quotes.
18 T.H. Redford, diary, 7 June 1915. AWM PR85/064
19 T.S. Austin, 'History of the 8th ALH Regiment'. AWM MSS0351
20 White, diary
21 Austin, 'History of the 8th ALH Regiment'
22 Austin, 'History of the 8th ALH Regiment'
23 Noel Carthew, *Voices from the Trenches: Letters to home*, New Holland, Chatswood, NSW, 2002, p. 44

Chapter 8: Walker's Ridge and Russell's Top

1 C.E.W. Bean, *The Story of Anzac from 4 May, 1915, to the Evacuation of the Gallipoli Peninsula*, vol. 2: Official History of Australia in the War of 1914–1918, Angus and Robertson, Sydney, 1924, p. 617

2 Bean, letter to Kent Hughes, 8 June 1928. AWM 38 3DRL 6673 Item 196

3 Antill, letter to brother, 11 March 1916. AWM 3DRL 6458

4 Bean, *The Story of Anzac*, vol. 2, p. 617

5 Hubert Foster, *Reorganisation*, Hugh Rees Ltd, London, 1920, p. 246

6 M. Reynell (Mrs), letter to C.E.W. Bean, official history biographical and research files. AWM 43

7 *The Roll of Honour*, London Stamp Exchange Ltd., London, p. 304

8 A. H. Borthwick, letter to parents, 14 July 1915. AWM PRO1729

9 After surviving the battle of The Nek, Deeble was sent to Britain, where he mostly commanded training camps; he was briefly commanding officer of the 48th Battalion.

10 A.H. White, diary

11 W. Cameron, diary. AWM 1DRL 185

12 P. Callary, letter, 8 July 1915. AWM 1DRL 178

13 W.A. McConnan, letter to father, 24 August 1915. AWM PR01577

14 Miss N.M. McConnan, South Yarra, Victoria, letter to Australian War Memorial, 18 January 1985. AWM 315 232/3/8

15 W. Cameron, diary

16 G.F.G. Wieck, letter to official historian. AWM 38 3DRL 7953 Item 27

17 Aubrey Herbert, *Mons, Anzac and Kut*, Hutchinson and Co., London, n.d., p. 152

18 A.H. White, diary

19 Captain Francis Beamish, from the field ambulance, was promptly appointed to replace Campbell.

20 White, diary

21 T.A. Kidd, diary

22 H. Foss, diary

23 A.J. Love, letter to Brazier, 13 July 1915. AWM 1 DRL 147

24 W. Robinson, letter to official historian, 16 May 1924. AWM 38 3DRL 8042 Item 25

25 Antill papers. AWM 3DRL 3607

26 Frederick Howard, *Kent Hughes: A biography of Colonel The Hon. Sir Wilfrid Kent Hughes*, Macmillan, South Melbourne, 1972, p. 15

27 Arthur Olden, 'Celebrities of the AIF; Lt-Col. T.J. Todd', *Reveille*, 30 May 1931, p. 9

28 Olden, 'Celebrities of the AIF; Lt-Col. T.J. Todd', *Reveille*, 30 May 1931, p. 9

Chapter 9: The New Offensive

1 T.S. Austin, 'History of the 8th ALH Regiment'

2 W. Cameron, diary

3 Brudenell White, *Reveille*, 1 May 1935, p. 17

4 T.H. Redford, diary

5 T.H. Darley, *With the Ninth Light Horse in the Great War*, Hassell Press, Adelaide, 1924, p. 14

6 Cameron, diary

7 'Consideration for an attack on Baby 700', War diary, 3rd ALH Brigade, August 1915. AWM 4 Item 10/3/7

8 A.H. White, diary

9 J. Antill, letter to brother, 12 October 1915. AWM 3DRL 6458
10 J.G. Hughes, 'Celebrities of the AIF; Sir Alexander Godley', *Reveille,* 1 May 1935, p. 8
11 Christopher Pugsley, *Gallipoli: The New Zealand Story*, Hodder and Stoughton, Auckland, 1984, p. 226
12 C. Reynell, diary, entry for 2 August 1915
13 Reynell, diary, entry for 4 August 1915
14 T.S. Austin, 'History of the 8th ALH Regiment'. AWM MSS0351
15 C.C.D. Pinnock, letter to father, 15 August 1915. AWM 1 DRL 547
16 Brazier, letter to Bean, 19 March 1931. AWM 3DRL 7953 Item 27
17 'Operational Order No. 1', War diary, 3rd ALH Brigade, August 1915. AWM 4 Item 10/3/7
18 W. Robinson, letter to official historian, 16 May 1924. AWM 38 3DRL 8042 Item 25
19 Letter, 5 August 1915, Borthwick papers. Keith Borthwick was killed; Alex survived only to be frightfully wounded in France 12 months later.
20 A. Meldrum, letter to mother, 12 August 1915, unattributed newspaper cutting (author)
21 C.E.W. Bean, *The Story of Anzac from 4 May, 1915, to the Evacuation of the Gallipoli Peninsula*, vol. 2: Official History of Australia in the War of 1914–1918, Angus and Robertson, Sydney, 1924, p. 610
22 Bean, *The Story of Anzac*, vol. 2, p. 610
23 *The Roll of Honour*, London Stamp Exchange Ltd, London, p. 348
24 H.J. Nugent, letter to mother, 12 August 1915, unattributed newspaper cutting (author)
25 T.H. Redford, diary (McGrath addendum)
26 *Ballarat Courier*, 4 October 1915, p. 4
27 J. Antill, letter to official historian. AWM 38 3DRL 7953 Item 25
28 Antill, letter to official historian
29 Antill, letter to official historian

Chapter 10: 'Come on boys. Come on. Come on.'

1 C.C.D. Pinnock, letter to father, 15 August 1915. AWM 1DRL/547
2 C.E.W. Bean, *The Story of Anzac from 4 May, 1915, to the Evacuation of the Gallipoli Peninsula*, vol. 2: Official History of Australia in the War of 1914–1918, Angus and Robertson, Sydney, 1924, p. 612
3 W. Robinson, letter to official historian, 9 May 1924
4 G. Hore, letter to mother, unattributed newspaper cutting (author)
5 W.S. Kent Hughes, letter to official historian, 29 February 1924. AWM 38 3DRL 8042 Item 25
6 C.E.W. Bean, *The All Australia Memorial: A historical record of national effort during the Great War*, British-Australian Publishing Service, Melbourne, 1919, p. 104
7 Bean, *The Story of Anzac*, vol. 2, p. 614
8 Pinnock, letter, 15 August 1915
9 T.H. Redford, diary (undated addendum)
10 Account in J. Beacham Kiddle (ed.), *War Services of Old Melbournians, 1914–1918* Arbuckle, Waddell Pty Ltd, Melbourne, 1923, p. 138
11 Interview with Lionel Simpson of Bacchus Marsh, Victoria, Canberra, 20 August 1984
12 Hore, letter to mother (n.d.)
13 Quoted in Peter Burness, 'Tragedy of two brothers', *Wartime*, 54, April 2011, p. 57
14 W. Cameron, diary. AWM 1DRL 185
15 Interview with H.D. Dean, of Ballarat, Victoria, Canberra, 20 August 1984

16 W. Robinson, letter to official historian, 16 May 1924
17 *The Roll of Honour,* London Stamp Exchange Ltd, London, p. 348
18 *The Roll of Honour,* p. 348
19 Report to 3ALH Bde HQ, 7 August 1915. War Diary 3 ALH Brigade AWM 4
20 A. Crawford, interview with Ian Jones, 25 April 1972. Transcript held by Mr I. Jones
21 A. Meldrum, letter to mother, 12 August 1915, unattributed newspaper cutting (author)
22 W. McConnan, letter to father, 15 August 1915. AWM PR01577
23 V.K. Boynton, letter to sister, *Riverina Recorder*, 1 December 1915

Chapter 11: The Decision

1 T.S. Austin, 'History of the 8th ALH Regiment'. AWM MSS0351
2 W.D. Oliver, letter to official historian, 30 March 1924. AWM 38 3DRL 7953 Item 27
3 Trooper G.T. Grant, details in AWM 131 Roll of Honour circulars, 1914–18 War, Item 252/42
4 *Western Mail* (Perth), 5 November 1936. The correspondent identifies himself as '172 (10th Light Horse)': this regimental number had been allotted to Corporal Evan Bain.
5 N. Brazier, report accompanying letter to official historian. AWM 38 3DRL 7953, Item 27
6 John Hamilton, *Goodbye Cobber, God Bless You*, Macmillan, Sydney, 2004, p. 309
7 Alf Batchelder, 'Sport and war', *The Yorker*, Journal of the Melbourne Cricket Club Library, issue 41, Autumn 2010, p. 5
8 J. Antill, letter to official historian. AWM 38 3DRL 7953 Item 27
9 War diary, 3rd ALH Brigade. AWM 4 Item 10/3/7
10 H. Foss, diary. AWM 1 DRL 298
11 N. Brazier, report accompanying letter to official historian. AWM 3DRL 7953 Item 27
12 N. Brazier, letter to official historian, 7 March 1924. AWM 3DRL 8042 Item 25
13 Bean, *The Story of Anzac*, vol. 2, p. 619
14 C.E.W. Bean, *The Story of Anzac from 4 May, 1915, to the Evacuation of the Gallipoli Peninsula*, Vol. 2: Official History of Australia in the War of 1914–1918, Angus and Robertson, Sydney, 1924, pp.619–20
15 T. A. Kidd, "diary" (rewritten "from memory"), entry for 7 August 1915. AWM PR82/137
16 Ric Throssell, *For Valour*, Currency Press, Sydney, 1976, p. xxiv
17 Peter Liddle, *Men of Gallipoli*, Allen Lane, London, 1976, p. 207
18 Peter Burness, 'Tragedy of two brothers', *Wartime*, 54, April 2011, p. 57
19 C. Reynell, diary 10 August 1915
20 Bean, *The Story of Anzac*, vol. 2, p. 620
21 Bean, *The Story of Anzac*, vol. 2, p. 620
22 N Brazier, diary, entry for 13 October 1914. 1DRL/0147
23 National Archives of Australia, Series B2455, Andrew Percival Rowan file
24 *West Australian*, 23 August 1915
25 Recommendation files for honours and awards, 1914–18 war. AWM 28
26 M. O'Donoghue, letter. Unattributed newspaper cutting (author)
27 List of recommendations, 3rd ALH Brigade Despatch dated 29 April 1916. AWM 28 Recommendation files for honours and awards, 1914–18 War.
28 List of recommendations, 3rd ALH Brigade Despatch dated 29 April 1916
29 C.W. Ashburner, interview with official historian. AWM 38 3DRL 606 Item 32
30 W. Robinson, letter to official historian, 16 May 1924. AWM 38 3DRL 8042 Item 25
31 T.S. Austin, 'History of the 8th ALH Regiment'. AWM MSS0351

32 Interview with E.C. MacGregor, 20 August 1984
33 T.H. Redford, diary (McGrath addendum)
34 W.A. McConnan, letter to father, 15 August 1915. AWM PR 01577
35 C.C.D. Pinnock, letter to father, 15 August 1915
36 Jeffrey Grey, *Australian Brass: The career of Lieutenant General Sir Horace Robertson*, Cambridge University Press, Oakleigh, Vic., 1992, p. 12
37 Arthur Olden, 'Celebrities of the AIF; Lt-Col. T.J. Todd', *Reveille*, 30 May 1931, p. 38
38 M.B. Higgins, letter to father, 14 August 1915. The letter is included in a photograph album attributed to Higgins, held in AWM Photograph, Sound and Film collection.
39 See *Appendix*.
40 McConnan, letter to father, 24 August 1915. AWM PR 01577

Chapter 12: The Aftermath of Battle

1 A.C.N. Olden, *Westralian Cavalry in the War: The story of the Tenth Light Horse Regiment, AIF*, Alexander McCubbin, Melbourne, 1921, p. 50
2 Olden, *Westralian Cavalry in the War*, p. 50
3 Reynell, diary
4 3rd ALH Brigade, Routine Order BM 360, 9 August 1915
5 Actual casualties were about 400.
6 W. Cameron, diary. AWM 1DRL185
7 P.I. Callary, letter, 22 August 1915. AWM 1DRL 178
8 Temporary Second Lieutenant Henry Whitehead was reported to have survived the charge only to be killed within a few hours by shrapnel.
9 After the war Major Love was discharged in Egypt to enable him to join the civil administration in Palestine.
10 Olden, *Westralian Cavalry in the War*, p. 51
11 Norman Worrall, letter to his father, 5 July 1915. Unattributed newspaper cutting (author)
12 C.E.W. Bean, despatch of 27 September 1915, Commonwealth of Australia Gazette, 16 November 1915 (reprinted in Military Order No. 726/1915)
13 V.B. Portman, quoted in *Stand To*, Canberra, February 1955, p. 8
14 Chistopher Pugsley, *Gallipoli: The New Zealand story*, Hodder and Stoughton, Auckland, 1990, p. 275
15 3rd ALH Brigade, message, 24 August 1915. AWM 25, Item 367/30
16 Brazier, diary
17 Brazier, papers
18 Antill, diary
19 *Hamilton Spectator*, 28 August 1915
20 L.L. Robson, *The First AIF: A study in recruitment, 1914–18*, Melbourne University Press, Melbourne, 1982, p. 72
21 C.E.W. Bean, despatch in *Commonwealth of Australia Gazette*, 30 September 1915 (reprinted with Military order No. 619/1915)
22 Brian Lewis, *Our War*, Penguin, Ringwood, Vic., 1981, p. 158
23 *The Roll of Honour*, London Stamp Exchange Ltd., London, p. 239
24 *The Roll of Honour*, p. 148
25 Trooper M. Larkin. AWM 131, Item 291/13
26 Quoted in Nettie Palmer, *Henry Bourne Higgins: A memoir*, George G. Harrap and Co., Sydney, 1931, p. 233

27 Papers of Sir Keith Arthur Murdoch, 'Gallipoli letter from Keith Arthur Murdoch to Andrew Fisher, 1915' (manuscript), p. 20. NLA MS2823
28 C.E.W. Bean, *The Story of Anzac from 4 May, 1915, to the Evacuation of the Gallipoli Peninsula*, Vol. 2: Official History of Australia in the War of 1914–1918, Angus and Robertson, Sydney, 1924, p. 632. The 4th Brigade, commanded by Brigadier General John Monash, was to capture Hill 971, but had to abandon the attack after it became exhausted, lost and suffering casualties.

Chapter 13: Reflection

1 C.B.B. White, letter to C.E.W. Bean (nd). AWM 38 3DRL 7954 Item 27 (Part 3)
2 W.R. Birdwood, order contained in 3ALH Brigade war diary. AWM 4 Item 10/3/7
3 C.E.W. Bean, *The Story of Anzac from 4 May, 1915, to the Evacuation of the Gallipoli Peninsula*, vol. 2: Official History of Australia in the War of 1914–18, Angus and Robertson, Sydney, 1924, p. 464
4 C.E.W. Bean, *The Story of Anzac*, vol. 2, p. 606
5 Report on the operations against Sari Bair Ridge, 6–10 August 1915. AWM 38 3DRL 7953 Item 27
6 Antill, letter to official historian (attachment to Bean letter, 17 June 1931). AWM 38 3DRL 7953 Item 27
7 W. Kent Hughes, letter to official historian, 29 February 1924. AWM 38 3DRL 6673/196
8 Aubrey Herbert, *Mons, Anzac and Kut*, Hutchison, London, n.d., p. 141
9 *The Roll of Honour*, London Stamp Exchange Ltd, London, p. 239
10 Talbot Hobbs, letter to official historian, 22 February 1923. AWM 38 3DRL 8047 Item 25. George Johnston was a citizen soldier who rose to command 2nd Division Artillery before becoming Administrator in New Guinea and reaching rank of major general.
11 Melbourne *Argus*, 29 December 1924
12 F. Hughes, letter to Australian official historian (attachment to Bean letter, 17 June 1931). AWM 38 3DRL 7953 Item 27
13 Antill, letter to official historian (attachment to Bean letter, 17 June 1931)
14 In 1915 Hughes was promoted to brigadier general (General Order No. 566/1915).
15 Melbourne *Argus*, 29 December 1924
16 Antill, papers. AWM 3DRL 6458
17 Bean, letter to Kent Hughes, 8 June 1928. AWM 3DRL 6673 Item 196
18 J.T.H. Aram, letter to family, 25 April 1916. AWM PR84/87

Chapter 14: Remembrance

1 *The Age*, 29 July 1991
2 W. Perry, 'The Victorian Horse Artillery', *Victorian Historical Magazine*, vol. 43, no. 1, p. 754
3 Rose Antill de Warren, 'A daughter's tribute to her father', *Reveille*, 1 June 1937, p. 20
4 Veronica McGowan, letter to author, 27 June 2000
5 Amy Lambert, *Thirty Years of an Artist's Life: The career of G.W. Lambert ARA*, Society of Artists, Sydney, 1938, p. 104
6 *Australian War Memorial Museum: A guidebook for the use of visitors*, Government Printer, Sydney, 1926, p. 14
7 Imperial War Graves Commission, *The War Graves of the British Empire – Gallipoli*, The Nek Cemetery, Cemetery Index No. G1.9, London, 1928, p. 53

8 Neville Browning and Ian Gill, *Gallipoli to Tripoli*, privately published, Perth, 2011, p. 115

9 Phil Taylor and Pam Cupper, *Gallipoli: A battlefield guide*, Kangaroo Press, Sydney, 1989, p. 191

INDEX

 **e-newsletter**

If you love books as much as we do, why not subscribe to our weekly e-newsletter?

As a subscriber, you'll receive special offers and discounts, be the first to hear of our exciting upcoming titles, and be kept up to date with book tours and author events. You will also receive unique opportunities exclusive to subscribers – and much more!

To subscribe in Australia or from any other country except New Zealand, visit
www.exislepublishing.com.au/newsletter-sign-up

For New Zealand, visit
www.exislepublishing.co.nz/newsletter-subscribe